Speed Reading

How to Master Your Attention and Focus Triple Your Reading Speed

(The Ultimate Guide to Master Fast Reading and Increase Memory)

Loren McMann

Published By **Jordan Levy**

Loren McMann

Speed Reading: How to Master Your Attention and Focus Triple Your Reading Speed (The Ultimate Guide to Master Fast Reading and Increase Memory)

ISBN 978-1-998927-13-5

Legal & Disclaimer

The information contained in this book is not designed to replace or take the place of any form of medicine or professional medical advice. The information in this book has been provided for educational & entertainment purposes only.

The information contained in this book has been compiled from sources deemed reliable, and it is accurate to the best of the Author's knowledge; however, the Author cannot guarantee its accuracy and validity and cannot be held liable for any errors or omissions. Changes are periodically made to this book. You must consult your doctor or get professional medical advice before using any of the suggested remedies, techniques, or information in this book.

Table Of Contents

Chapter 1: Lets Get Speed Reading

The time period "tempo analyzing" refers to a manner of analyzing that lets a person examine at a substantially quicker tempo. Speed studying can be performed through selectively reading unique terms or phrases which can be associated with the reading fabric, through skimming or via distinct tempo studying techniques that you may discover later in the e book.

While there can be an inverse correlation amongst reading pace and comprehension level, i.E., pinnacle of the road comprehension is done at decrease studying speeds, you may nevertheless advantage tons from studying a way to pace have a look at. Some of the blessings you may revel in at the same time as you discover ways to tempo read consist of:

1)Spend Less Time Reading and More Time Learning: When you're able to pace-take a look at, you obtained't take as a super deal time as everyday simply to apprehend the crucial factors of what you're seeking to read. This technique you'll have the ability to analyze more matters given the identical term and you'll be capable of get greater topics completed.

2)Greater Mental Focus: A brilliant chunk of tempo studying is focusing at the phrases you're studying on a given frame of textual content in addition to their groupings and your reading pace. As you discover ways to speed study, you'll inadvertently learn how to reputation higher and come to be greater aware of what you're doing.

3)Better Memory: The capability to examine extra with quite appropriate comprehension stage can help you memorize and preserve extra topics for your thoughts compared to studying at your contemporary, ordinary pace. The extra you can observe and recognize in a given period of time, the extra you'll be capable of keep in your memory.

4)Improved Problem-Solving Abilities: When you're able to have a look at and recognize extra inside a selected time frame in evaluation to what you can do inside the period in-between, you'll be able to analyze extra hacks that assist you to treatment regular challenges.

5)Higher Grades: If you're a scholar, being able to observe and apprehend more in a given duration of time assist you to apprehend more of your faculty's education higher. This will can help you get higher grades in phrases of taking your checks.

6)Improved Decision-Making Abilities: Finally, when you're able to look at and study more new and beneficial topics, you can gain more useful statistics and increase your inventory records. The extra you have got were given on your stock information, the extra selection-making options you can have, which assist you to make wiser picks within the future.

What It Is and What It's Not

Before proceeding similarly, you'll want to get the skinny on pace reading so that you can appreciate it for what it actually is and avoid unrealistic expectations about it.

Speed studying is a very beneficial knowledge that will let you examine the primary factors or favored mind provided in a given body of text, specially while you're below time stress. For example, your boss' boss all of sudden asks you to provide the final inner audit file to the company's Board of Directors after lunch, in lieu of your boss who had to name in sick due to the flu.

Unless you're the simplest who organized the document, you'll have constrained time to digest the entirety in the document. But because maximum displays to top manipulate are commonly immoderate-level, which means they best want to understand the overall blessings and implications of what's being provided, you could attention on identifying and know-how the number one elements and sub-elements of said record in the constrained hours you're given. For this, tempo reading is proper. Playstation ... This is why I in my view learnt a manner to hurry observe

Another situation much like the aforementioned one in which tempo studying can show to be very useful is writing massive content material material, whether or no longer it's for a blog, a book, or a document. Freelance writers who want to fulfill particular phrase-depend variety quotas and time limits on a each day and weekly foundation are a number of the exquisite pace readers around. Often times, they write on a extensive variety of topics and genres, plenty of which may be sudden to them. The simplest manner they could crank out the required type of phrase contents inside limited durations of time is through being able to rapid get the overall thoughts out of the content fabric fabric they're in a position to research.

Speed studying isn't a subject mastery tool. As stated earlier, there's an inverse correlation among most reliable analyzing comprehension and analyzing speed. This technique in case you need a totally deep facts or whole mastery of a given topic, you can't come up with the money for to genuinely understand the primary thoughts of related contents. You'll want to gradual down enough to system each little bit of records within the texts you examine.

A high-quality example could be taking computer programming training. Speed reading will will let you put together in your classes by means of presenting you with a extraordinary statistics of the overall thoughts if you want to be noted in the commands, that might feature useful getting to know anchors or wireframes. These learning anchors or wireframes will let you relate new and unusual records to something you already apprehend, which help you understand them better.

Mastery requires knowledge nuances of unique terminologies and ideas. The phrase "era" is a fairly complex term applied in software program software improvement, which a scholar together with you who's simply analyzing laptop programming might not truly apprehend. When you encounter this term in pace reading, you can't come up with the money for to really keep analyzing. Either you can need to prevent and research what the time period manner or spotlight it so that you can research what it technique in a while. Regardless of your desire, you may ought to depend upon some element extra than pace reading to recognise laptop programming.

Now that you understand what tempo analyzing is and isn't always, you'll be in a extraordinary feature to understand whilst to apply it on your most effective studying results.

Chapter 2: The Power of Your Brain

Before we get into the info of tempo analyzing, it's important to recognize how the mind works for the duration of ordinary and speed reading, and the way it stores records. This will assist you to higher use the velocity analyzing techniques you'll examine later and to comprehend them extra. I promised a "No Fluff" guide and that's what I plan to deliver. I even have simplest protected records I deem relevant to apprehend why the techniques work. I accept as genuine with facts this statistics will help you spot why schooling those everyday techniques can paintings after you apprehend how the mind reacts to them.

How the Brain Processes Normal Reading

When a person reads discovered materials, there are 3 tactics with the useful resource of which the thoughts methods statistics received from such materials. These are:

1)Visual Information Processing: In this step, the eyes visually approach the data from the phrases (analyzing) and the thoughts strategies the photographs of the phrases. The mind acknowledges and registers the ones snap shots below seen facts processing.

2)Acoustical Information Processing: During this step, the thoughts facts the seen facts it has processed as an acoustic message or voice in the language that it knows, e.G., English, Japanese, Spanish, and so forth. During acoustical information processing, a person "hears" the processed phrases within the thoughts and reads terms exactly as they sound at the same time as stated. Here, the mind acoustically encodes the facts that became processed visually earlier. This can occasionally be acoustically processed in the voice of the writer if that may be a individual or recognize as although they're truly speakme proper away to you.

3)Meaning or Semantic Processing: In this final studying-information processing step, the mind analyzes visually and acoustically-processed data in the acquainted language / voice. The thoughts additionally extracts the which means of such information on this degree, which permits it to acquire large facts from the phrases examine.

How the Brain Functions During Speed Reading

As noted in advance, a person who makes use of pace analyzing can observe and research significantly more compared to everyday-paced reading. Anybody can check this skills and may draw near it by the usage of the usage of working towards constantly. When someone velocity reads, that man or woman can modify how the mind competencies at the equal time as studying. Basically, pace reading improves or optimizes the human thoughts's facts processing capacities associated with studying.

When a person reads commonly or at ordinary pace, that person can test anywhere from one hundred eighty to 230 terms every minute. A man or woman who tempo reads can have a look at as masses as 900 phrases every minute!

How does the human thoughts do this? By the use of precise pace analyzing techniques that permit it to adjust its visual and acoustical records techniques because of this. You will test the ones techniques inside the succeeding chapters.

How the Brain Memorizes Information

We can outline reminiscence as an ongoing approach that recruits many regions of the body, consisting of the mind. Contrary to what many humans suppose, memory isn't a physical thing or organ within the frame like the brain or the kidneys.

The time period "reminiscences" speak over with highbrow opinions or documents of things that have befell in the beyond, which includes our recollections of beyond studies. Memories start with the senses, which might be the technique through which we revel in topics, e.G., sight, sound, contact, flavor, and fragrance.

Our thoughts chooses which the various many wonderful enjoy-related facts we gather on a each day basis may be saved as reminiscences. If the mind doesn't clear out which facts ought to be stored, it will overload itself and will no longer be able to feature in any respect. That's why the mind has to selectively save facts as memories.

The hippocampus is the primary part of the brain that procedures recollections. Many experts maintain in thoughts that statistics that the hippocampus strategies is stored in unique regions of the mind's cerebral cortex, a.Ok.A., the "gray keep in mind quantity." This is how your mind will hold the crucial records even as you pace examine.

When the thoughts accumulates memories, it moreover determines how essential saved recollections are. To keep away from being overloaded, the mind continuously filters and prioritizes processed information. The mind places records it deems desired for a brief time frame, e.G., a cellular smartphone quantity for fast and one-time dialing, in a "folder" known as brief-time period reminiscence.

The intellectual folder known as quick-time period reminiscence has very constrained garage area. Experts accept as true with that most people can most effective keep as a lot as a maximum of seven gadgets in brief-term memory for no longer than 30 seconds. One of the techniques to boom the live of data in brief-term memory is repetition.

The mind transfers the most essential portions of statistics from quick-term to prolonged-time period reminiscence. Intentional or unintentional repetition ought to make the thoughts assign a super diploma of significance to particular gadgets in brief-term memory and compel the mind to head to and fro it to the prolonged-term reminiscence highbrow folder. The degree of emotional effect specific research offer can have an effect on the degree of importance that the mind will assign to them, which subsequently determines whether or not or no longer they'll be transferred to the prolonged-term memory folder.

The correct information is that lengthy-term reminiscence isn't confined thru manner of the equal storage space obstacles as short-term memory is. Many scientists count on that the prolonged-time period reminiscence has neither limits as regards to the type of recollections saved nor the period of time recollections are saved. Think approximately it: some of your most unforgettable memories are the ones from some years in the past, along with children ones.

The Mind's Ability to Absorb Imagery and Ideas

The thoughts absorbs and maintains facts in unique strategies. And in terms of memory retention, there is a motive for the saying that a picture paints a thousand phrases. Images help us studies some component better, draw close our awareness and hobby a good buy much less complex, offer an purpose behind rather complex mind higher, and inspire us.

But why are we able to reply a bargain better to visible stimuli as compared to others? The high-quality answer is probably that we're seen beings, with a remarkable bite of our mind focused on seen processing. Compared to different kinds of data, our mind methods visible records (pictures) at a far faster rate. Consider the following:

1)Read this sentence; "Stephen Curry made the sport winning three-component shot for the Golden State Warriors in competition to the Houston Rockets." and

2)Look at a photo of Stephen Curry launching a three-component shot with James Harden on his face and a image of the game clock with most effective a 2d final.

If you go together with number one, it'll take you as a minimum 2 to a few seconds to manner and recognize the facts. But with good sized range 2, it'll without a doubt take you a second. That's how rapid visible data processing is.

When you've got a study memory improvement books, one of the maximum endorsed techniques for without problems committing a particular piece of facts to lengthy-time period reminiscence is by way of the usage of painting an absurd picture of it inside the mind. Why? According to memory specialists, the crazier the photograph is, the extra it'll stand out and the more hard it'll be to neglect it.

I preference you could see how effective your thoughts absolutely is and the manner it'll effects shop the information brought to it via analyzing and the manner, with a piece of workout, you could tempo this method up with out dropping any of the preferred information.

Chapter 3: Determine Your Reading Speed

Now that you recognise how effective the human thoughts is and the manner it abilties while analyzing, it's time to get the charge reading ball rolling. And the number one essential step is to decide your modern-day reading pace.

Why do this? It's due to the reality facts and recording your analyzing pace will give you an objective basis for which to determine your development. And based totally on the modifications to your recorded reading velocity, you can make the crucial changes if needed.

It's one aspect to mention, "I enjoy my studying pace has expanded enormously within the closing three weeks." It's a few other to mention, "In the last three weeks, I was able to boom my analyzing speed from three hundred terms-in line with-minute to 500 phrases-in keeping with-minute!"

Reading speed has three factors: common tempo, processing pace, and memorizing pace. Average speed refers to real amount of phrases you can look at in keeping with minute, regardless in case you're able to apprehend or memorize the things you study. Here's the way to diploma your common pace (AS):

1)Choose a web web page from a e-book or a selected studying fabric or use the text supplied on the stop of this financial ruin (word depend is furnished subsequent to textual content).

2)Count the kind of phrases of that web web page or reading cloth.

three)Using a timer, document how extended it takes you to finish reading your preferred material.

four)Divide the quantity of phrases of your selected studying material via the use of the sort of seconds it took you to finish reading it and multiply it with the aid of 60 to get your

AS, expressed as terms-in keeping with-minute (WPM).

The second element of reading tempo is comprehension, it's miles measured as processing speed or (PS). While the reason of tempo studying is to have a look at speedy, it received't endorse lots in case you're now not able to definitely make sense of what you have got were given have been given take a look at. Measuring PS requires answering a tough and speedy of questions after studying a chunk of textual content, which might be prepared by manner of a person else to ensure integrity of questions. The percent of questions answered correctly will determine the PS score, i.E., eight out of 10 questions spoke back effectively way a PS score of eighty%. Obviously you may not have a person to try this so you can sincerely consider what you in reality examine and supply a short description of it to your self. How easy you find this could determine your comprehension.

The very last component of analyzing tempo is memorizing pace (MS), which refers to how many terms you can study and understand every minute. It's essentially a mixture of the AS (studying tempo) and PS (comprehension).

MS is computed through multiplying the AS via the PS. If your AS is three hundred WPM and your PS is eighty%, then your MS is:

three hundred wpm X eighty% = 240 WPM

The final aim of velocity studying is every pace and comprehension. That's why as lots as possible, you need to use MS as your barometer for pace studying improvement. However, it may be difficult or maximum inconvenient to degree progress with MS as it calls for the assist of every other character to create questions to be accomplished successfully with the aid of the usage of the usage of which to degree your PS. Also, comprehension is a topic that could take a few different entire ebook to cover. Therefore, this ebook will interest in particular on AS.

To degree your baseline AS, study the subsequent textual content, time yourself, and calculate your AS.

Treasure Island — Robert Louis Stevenson — (605 Words)

As rapid as Silver disappeared, the captain, who had been carefully looking him, grew to become within the direction of the indoors of the residence and located no longer a person folks at his submit but Gray. It was the number one time we had ever visible him angry.

"Quarters!" he roared. And then, as we slunk decrease back to our places, "Gray," he stated, "I'll positioned your call in the log; you have stood by means of the usage of your duty like a seaman. Mr. Trelawney, I'm surprised at you, sir. Doctor, I idea you had worn the king's coat! If that come to be the way you served at Fontenoy, sir, you'll had been higher on your berth."

The medical doctor's watch have been all again at their loopholes, the rest had been busy loading the spare muskets, and simply everybody with a crimson face, you will be high great, and a flea in his ear, because the pronouncing is.

The captain seemed on for a while in silence. Then he spoke.

"My lads," he stated, "I've given Silver a broadside. I pitched it in red-heat on cause; and in advance than the hour's out, as he said, we shall be boarded. We're outnumbered, I want not tell you that, but we fight in secure haven; and, a minute in the past, I must have stated we fought with problem. I've no way of doubt that we are capable of drub them if you choose."

Then he went the rounds, and located, as he said, that each one changed into smooth.

On the two quick components of the house, east and west, there have been handiest loopholes; on the south side wherein the porch have become, two all over again; and on the north facet, 5. There grow to be a spherical score of muskets for the seven dad and mom; the firewood were constructed into 4 piles—tables, you will in all likelihood say—one approximately the middle of every problem, and on each of those tables a few ammunition and four loaded muskets have been laid geared up to the hand of the defenders. In the center, the cutlasses lay ranged.

"Toss out the fireplace," stated the captain; "the relax is beyond, and we should now not have smoke in our eyes."

The iron hearth basket became carried physical out through Mr. Trelawney, and the embers smothered amongst sand.

"Hawkins hasn't had his breakfast. Hawkins, help your self, and again for your located as a lot as eat it," persevered Captain Smollett. "Lively, now, my lad; you may want it earlier than you have got done. Hunter, serve out a round of brandy to all arms."

And whilst this changed into taking place the captain finished, in his very own thoughts, the plan of the protection.

"Doctor, you may take the door," he resumed. "See and don't disclose yourself; preserve inside, and hearth through the porch. Hunter, take the east facet, there. Joyce, you stand thru the west, my man. Mr. Trelawney, you are the brilliant shot—you and Gray will take this prolonged north factor, with the 5 loopholes; it is in which the chance is. If they will rise as much as it, and hearth in upon us through our personal ports, things could begin to appearance grimy. Hawkins, neither you nor I are plenty account at the capturing; we are going to stand with the resource of to load and go through a hand."

As the captain had stated, the take a seat returned became past. As fast due to the fact the solar had climbed above our girdle of wood, it fell with all its force upon the clearing and drank up the vapors at a draught. Soon the sand changed into baking, and the resin melting within the logs of the blockhouse. Jackets and coats have been flung apart; shirts had been thrown open at the neck and rolled as a whole lot as the shoulders; and we stood there, every at his positioned up, in a fever of warmth and tension.

Chapter 4: Peripheral Vision

One of the most important elements of velocity studying is peripheral vision.

Basically, peripheral imaginative and prescient refers to your range of sight from one thing of your vision to the alternative, i.E., the vicinity of your imaginative and prescient beyond the center of your gaze. It represents the greatest location of your visual view and the broader your peripheral vision is, the greater subjects you may see in a single appearance.

Peripheral imaginative and prescient has three factors:

1)Near-Peripheral Vision, i.E., what you look at adjacent to the middle of your gaze;

2)Mid-Peripheral Vision, i.E., what you observe on the middle of your visual view; and

3)Far-Peripheral Vision, i.E., what you spot at the brink of your visual field.

A exquisite chunk of improving studying velocity is growing peripheral studying vision, i.E., the style of terms you may see in a difficult and rapid gaze. The more phrases you can see regular with gaze, the extra phrases you'll be capable of take a look at. And the greater terms you could study for the equal time period, the quicker you could have a take a look at.

You can find hundreds of peripheral imaginative and prescient improvement wearing activities online and it's far sincerely properly worth improving. I actually have include a few right proper right here to be able to have a pass at.

Peripheral Vision Improvement Exercise #1

1)Center your gaze at the celeb in the middle of the Picture 1-A under. Beginning with the letter "R," attempt to have a observe the letters surrounding the superstar without taking your gaze faraway from it.

2)Perform this workout as a great deal as five instances in keeping with consultation, some times each day. Give your eyes time to rest earlier than doing this exercise another time.

three)Move immediately to Picture 1-B while you're able to recognize each letter with out problem. Then to Picture 1-C

Picture 1-A

Description: Description: A close up of a logo Description automatically generated

Picture 1-B

Description: Description: A close up of a logo Description automatically generated

Picture 1-C

Description: Description: A close up of a device Description automatically generated

Peripheral Vision Improvement Exercise #2

This exercise modified into designed to enhance the potential of your eye muscle, that may translate into wider peripheral studying vision over time.

1)Begin through each status or sitting down and focusing your sight at once within the the front of you.

2)Stretch out both palms in your sides, such as you're developing a go with your body. Your palms want to be right away and perpendicular to the ground.

three)Make a thumbs-up sign with each hand and hold the pose at some degree inside the exercising.

four)Keeping your head constant and handling right now in advance of you, flow your eyes to the proper till you could see your proper thumb. If your eye muscle isn't that bendy however, simply flow it as a ways to the right as you may.

five)Move your eyes all of the way to the left until you see your left thumb or as an extended way as you could do it. That's one repetition. Perform nine more times to complete 1 set of 10 repetitions.

6)Do 3 gadgets of this workout constant with consultation and usually do not forget to keep your head constant and going thru without delay in advance in some unspecified time in the destiny of the actions.

Chapter 5: Important Speed Reading Principles

Now that you comprehend a manner to enhance your peripheral imaginative and prescient for velocity analyzing, it's time to investigate some of the maximum important mind for optimizing your studying tempo. While those aren't the speed reading strategies or methods in line with se, they really assist you make the maximum out of the techniques you'll have a look at inside the next financial ruin.

Minimize Sub-Vocalization

Also called auditory reassurance, it's one of the maximum ordinary studying conduct round. When someone sub-vocalizes, that man or woman mentally pronounces or says the terms being take a look at. And this addiction is one in every of the most important boundaries to optimizing reading velocity. This on my own helped my studying velocity mainly.

Most – if no longer all – speed studying programs claim to educate the way to absolutely get rid of studying sub-vocalization as really certainly one of their pinnacle reading pace development techniques. But clinical studies have demonstrated that's now not viable to actually cast off this dependancy. What is viable is notably decreasing this dependancy or minimizing it, which stays very beneficial in terms of improving studying velocity. Here are some practical methods you could reduce your tendency to sub-vocalize:

1)Guide Your Eyes: One of the foundational practices of powerful velocity reading is the usage of a few factor, e.G., a finger or an item, to guide the eyes even as analyzing. This may additionally furthermore appear a touch juvenile but it really works.

2)Distractions: One way to maintain your thoughts from mentally pronouncing the assets you study is by the usage of distracting it. However, the distraction shouldn't be that big or sturdy that it keeps you from clearly analyzing! A remarkable manner of distracting your mind enough to limit sub-vocalization without distracting you from analyzing is to bite gum as you're studying. Again, quite simple however this has labored for loads people and is well properly really worth a attempt.

three)Play Music: For me, a higher distraction than gum is tune. With song inside the statistics, the tendency to sub-vocalize can be decreased substantially. It can also help you concentrate higher on what you're studying. Just ensure you keep away from listening to track that has lyrics being sung, instrumental variations of songs with lyrics which you apprehend, and track that has a very robust emotional resonance with you. Personally, I find out that smooth, classical music works brilliant because it's no longer emotionally robust, it's calm, it commonly has no lyrics, and isn't mainstream sufficient to distract my mind from virtually reading. I still try this now on every occasion I look at four)Just Read Faster: By considerably developing the pace at which you test, you could restriction the tendency to sub-vocalize. How? By giving your mind a much harder time to capture up with sub-vocalization. Reading significantly faster than you generally do moreover can help you interest better due to the fact quicker studying calls for heightened attention and hobby.

Control Your Eye Movement

Ideally, eye movements whilst analyzing a e-book or some specific reading cloth must have the equal computerized responses as even as typing an electronic mail or the usage of a bike in a busy street. By enhancing eye motion in a selected way, you could restrict the sort of instances your eyes stop even as reading a line and the duration or length of each prevent.

Why is it essential to educate the attention to move in unique techniques for perfect analyzing speed? It's due to the fact eye moves impact our capacity to look at, which consist of the velocity at which we are able to have a have a look at.

Take for instance the fact that most humans agree with and claim that after they read, their eyes genuinely take a look at the print back and forth at a reasonably steady tempo in the course of pages. But the fact is, clinical research have confirmed that the eyes typically have a tendency to prevent and pass at numerous elements in a line of text, i.E., fixation, in a jerky movement in preference to flowing resultseasily to and fro.

When our eyes skip as we have a look at, they're not in reality "searching" at character words however as an opportunity, they simply glide from one prevent or fixation point to some other. And close to the time period spent reading every line of textual content, eye moves only account for 10% of the period. What this indicates is reading a line of text is crafted from numerous stops-and-is going or individual glances further to creating revel in of every look.

When it includes eye motion and reading tempo, you want to maintain this very vital precept in mind: the more fixations or stops-and-is going are made at the same time as studying a line of textual content, the time needed to make revel in of each fixation will increase too. Longer duration plus better frequency equals longer studying time, i.E., slower reading tempo. This is why your peripheral vision is so vital as a exquisite deal less fixations might be required. However, the proper fashion of fixations consistent with line of textual content and the duration of every fixation shouldn't be a one-duration-suits-all proposition. These would possibly rely upon the analyzing trouble or ease of the analyzing fabric. It's simplest herbal to take longer to approach odd or very technical reading substances, finally a slower reading pace.

The primary motive for analyzing unique texts ought to moreover be essential issues of analyzing pace. Reading an audited monetary record for capabilities of making an investment a big amount of money within the shares of a New York Stock Exchange-listed corporation should take a whole lot greater time in assessment to reading Dan Brown's bestselling novel The Da Vinci Code.

Minimize Regression

Regression refers to the studying dependancy of regularly going again to texts you already take a look at simply to ensure that you simply understood it. As you can see, often going decrease back to elements of a text you've already examine will slow down your reading pace due to commonplace repetitions. Until analyzing of regression at the same time as analyzing, I didn't comprehend in reality how a bargain I certainly did this.

There are techniques you could limit your tendency to regress at the same time as analyzing. First, you need to top your self up to recognition and read for a particular time period. This includes committing or blockading time for studying, i.E., reducing yourself off from all possible studying distractions like social media, email, or communications with one-of-a-type human beings. When you get distracted, you get thrown off from what you're analyzing, as a way to compel you to retrace your studying "steps" definitely to get once more into the flow.

Second, you could use some thing to cover the traces you've already check as you go with the go with the flow all of the way all the way all the way down to the lowest of the page you're reading. This may be a bit of white paper folded crosswise, which you can location on top of a e-book or an internet web page of material you're analyzing. As you end analyzing one line after each different, slide that folded paper on pinnacle of the traces you already study to prevent yourself from regressing. Do the same for succeeding pages you'll observe. You wont should do that for extended to train your self out of regressing.

Here's a top notch workout for growing the dependancy of minimizing regression:

1)Choose a physical e-book to examine, which should neither be essential or complex to look at. A novel is a remarkable instance of this kind of ebook.

2)Block off as a minimum half of-hour every day to do this exercise with none distractions or disruptions. This have to be the best issue you'll interest on for 1/2-hour.

three)In your mind, decide to sincerely cognizance at the exercise and not regressing to any previously completed texts or strains.

four)Use a white sheet of paper folded flow-smart to cowl lines you've already check at the same time as shifting down every web web page of the e-book you chose to take a look at.

The Chunking Method

Also referred to as chunk reading, chunking is a analyzing precept which says that the brilliant manner to make enjoy of texts is via manner of chunking or grouping them collectively. This is consistent with the reality that we don't look at "phrases" in step with se but clusters of phrases.

For example, that is much less complex to have a have a look at and apprehend among those ? Option A:

Stephen

Curry

Nailed

A

Killer

Crossover

Punctuated

By

A

30-foot

3-element

Shot.

Or Option B, which chunks phrases together as indicated via the use of the photo nailed a killer skip punctuated with the aid of a 30-foot three-factor shot.

Of course, Option B is the easier model to study and make feel of, right? Right!

Learning to Chunk Read Better

If this is the primary time you've heard of or positioned out approximately chunking, begin by way of way of way of analyzing how to "triple-bite" first. Here's a manner to do it:

1)Start thru deciding on an internet web page of posted text and dividing it into 3 factors through drawing 2 vertical lines at the internet net page to demarcate each of the equally-sized sections. The first line want to lessen off the number one 2 words of every line whilst the second one line want to reduce off the final phrases of each line.

2)Focus your eyes at the center phase of the web page best and simply let your peripheral vision see the primary 2 and the closing 2 terms of the road.

three)Focus handiest on studying the text in some of the two traces, i.E., the middle section. Don't thoughts the outer edges.

Once you've mastered the triple-chunking principle, the subsequent precept to understand is the double-chunking one. Here's how to exercise it:

1)Divide a web page of text into 2 equal halves thru manner of drawing a vertical line through the middle.

2)Read through the web page line by way of the use of way of line. Do this with the aid of glancing as soon as on each side of the road, treating every 1/2 of as although a whole unit.

three)With non-save you exercise, you'll learn how to reputation on the center line pleasant and be able to test whole strains through a far wider peripheral analyzing imaginative and prescient.

Chapter 6: Speed Reading Techniques

Now, allow's get to the pork of tempo analyzing. In this bankruptcy, we'll cowl the primary strategies you can learn how to use to optimize your analyzing velocity.

The Skimming and Scanning Method

These are seeking out recommendation from analyzing strategies that utilize REM or fast eye moves (no your now not going to have a sleep) together with key phrases. The primary intention of those 2 strategies is to move rapid via written texts thru figuring out key terms that screen the key thoughts or factors of a textual content.

What's the distinction many of the 2? Skimming is fast analyzing the goal of which is to offer you with a elegant evaluation of what you're studying, i.E., popular thoughts or points. Scanning refers to speedy reading, the purpose of this is to give you unique data.

Skimming offers you an idea of the overall statistics or thoughts within particular sections on the identical time as scanning gives you specific records or thoughts. To use a extra familiar evaluation, skimming is snorkeling at the equal time as scanning is diving.

When ought to you skim and while want to you experiment? You can use skimming for:

1)Reading earlier than analyzing a fabric, i.E., previewing a particular cloth;

2)Reading after analyzing a fabric, i.E., reviewing a particular material;

three)Getting the number one concept from an prolonged studying material you neither have the selection nor the time to examine notably; or

four)Finding resource materials for a studies paper, an editorial you're writing, or a ebook you're making plans to post.

Scanning is extra suitable while you're:

1)Looking for particular statistics in the course of research;

2)Studying topics which can be filled to the brim with statistics; or

three)To offer real useful resource in answering questions that require it.

How to Skim Read

You want to put together yourself to unexpectedly circulate through pages while seeking to skim. You might not have a look at every and each word within the text, however you may need to focus on typographical indicators like:

1)Numbered lists;

2)Bulleted lists;

three)Indented terms or paragraphs;

four)Bold-lettered or italicized phrases; and

5)Headings.

When skimming, you want to be seeking out abnormal phrases, names of places and people, nouns, dates, and key phrases and terms.

Here are the steps to test to discover ways to skim-study:

1)To get a well-known idea of techniques a reading material's critical mind or divided and sub-divided, undergo the monetary spoil evaluate (if any) or the table of contents.

2)Take short look at every of the bankruptcy's primary headings or each essential heading's sub-headings to get clues on what they're approximately. You can also look at the headings of tables and charts if supplied.

three)Read the whole beginning paragraph of every monetary wreck or important segment of the text you're reading.

4)Then, observe most effective the number one and last sentences of every succeeding paragraph.

5)For every succeeding paragraph, virtually examine the number one few terms of each sentence therein or search for the paragraph's maximum crucial idea great.

6)Stop and have a look at the boldfaced or italicized sentences with keywords right away.

7)If you be given as proper with that you've came upon a completely crucial idea, forestall skimming and observe the whole sentence to verify your hunch. Afterward, return to skim-analyzing.

eight)Where there are economic catastrophe or most important section summaries, study them.

Ideally, you need to undergo all of the above-mentioned steps. However, no person's ideal and we don't stay in a great global, i.E., there may be times it's not viable to accomplish that. When that takes place, certainly compromise through focusing fine at the economic damage overviews and summaries or unique available signs and symptoms like boldfaced or italicized terms, and so forth. Sometimes, the principle thoughts inner paragraphs aren't usually in the final and number one sentences so that you'll should make do with what's to be had like a financial ruin or phase summary or evaluate.

Skimming is truly a much quicker manner to observe via substances, it doesn't have to be completed at the equal speed. There are fine sections of text in that you'll need to slow down your skim-analyzing, on the facet of:

1)Skimming through introducing and concluding paragraphs;

2)Skimming via difficulty remember sentences;

3)When you come across an unusual word; and

four)When studying a very complex fabric.

How to Scan

Just like skimming, scanning consists of key phrases and typographical symptoms. The distinction lies within the objective, i.E., scanning isn't worried about getting a bird's eye view of a material however with finding and getting specific facts or statistics. Often times, scanning is the subsequent step after skimming via substances as skimming permits provide a elegant roadmap for a guided take a look at.

Here are the practical steps for getting to know a way to experiment:

1)Identify what it is you're looking for. Choose unique seek terms like key terms or key-phrase terms. When you test, you'll be a human-equal of Google and other engines like google.

2)When scanning, awareness on locating one search term at a time. If you've got several search phrases, check the fabric a couple of times in line with the shape of your are searching for phrases.

three)Allow your eyes to waft down pages rapid until you're able to locate your precise are seeking term.

4)As speedy as your eyes find any of your key phrases or terms, look at the texts proper now previous and following it to get an concept of its context and test for relevancy.

If you want to check substances with the aim of locating proper assist for answering questions, it could be much less complicated because of the truth one critical element of scanning's already been finished for you. Questions – through nature – already offer the critical element phrases you'll want for scanning. The last steps for scanning so that you can answer unique questions include:

1)Thoroughly take a look at the questions preceding to scanning your materials. From the questions themselves, you could discover your scanning key terms.

2)If you've got were given more than one questions to reply, check for solutions for one question at a time. Each experiment have to focus on answers to as a minimum one query splendid.

three)As speedy as you discover a key-word or phrase, test the texts proper away preceding and succeeding that key-phrase or phrase to test for relevancy.

four)Read the questions over again to recognise if the answers you find out are appropriate for answering your questions.

You can exercise skimming and scanning on this text:

Read the following 2 questions and notice if you can speedy solution them thru skimming and scanning:

1)Which century did the Magyars triumph over the u . S . A .?

2)What modified into the dream about?

Once you have got replied the previous questions. There are 2 extra after the text. Skim and test the whole text in advance than studying those and word if you could answer them.

Dracula – Bram Stoker – (605 Words)

In the population of Transylvania there are 4 great nationalities: Saxons in the South, and blended with them the Wallachs, who are the descendants of the Dacians; Magyars in the West, and Szekelys inside the East and North. I am going maximum of the latter, who declare to be descended from Attila and the Huns. This can be so, for even as the Magyars conquered the us of the usa inside the eleventh century they found the Huns settled in it. I test that each appeared superstition within the worldwide is collected into the horseshoe of the Carpathians as although it had been the middle of some kind of contemporary whirlpool; if so my stay may be very thrilling. (Mem., I want to ask the Count all about them.)

I did now not sleep well, even though my bed changed into cushty sufficient, for I had all styles of queer goals. There modified right into a canine howling all night under my window, which can also have had a few issue to do with it; or it could had been the paprika, for I had to drink up all of the water in my carafe, and become despite the fact that thirsty. Towards morning I slept and become awakened with the resource of the use of the non-stop knocking at my door, so I wager I need to were slumbering soundly then. I had for breakfast extra paprika, and a shape of porridge of maize flour which they stated modified into "mamaliga," and egg-plant filled with forcemeat, a completely wonderful dish, which they call "impletata." (Mem., get recipe for this moreover.) I had to hurry breakfast, for the teach commenced a touch before eight, or alternatively it must have completed so, for after rushing to the station at 7:30 I needed to sit down down inside the carriage for additonal than an hour in advance than we started out to move. It seems to me that the in addition east you pass the more unpunctual are the trains. What ought they to be in China?

All day lengthy we regarded to dawdle through a rustic which changed into entire of splendor of every type. Sometimes we observed little towns or castles at the top of steep hills which consist of we see in vintage missals; on occasion we ran with the beneficial aid of rivers and streams which seemed from the huge stony margin on each aspect of them to be mission to exceptional floods. It takes a whole lot of water and taking walks robust, to sweep the outside fringe of a river smooth. At each station there have been corporations of humans, every so often crowds, and in all styles of garb. Some of them were much like the peasants at domestic or the ones I noticed coming through France and Germany, with brief Jackets and spherical hats and home-made trousers; however others were very picturesque. The girls seemed quite, besides when you got close to them, but they have been very clumsy approximately the waist. They had all full white sleeves of a few type or distinctive, and most of them had large belts with hundreds of strips of some issue fluttering from them similar to the apparel in a ballet, however of path there had been petticoats beneath them. The strangest figures we noticed were the Slovaks, who have been more barbarian than the rest, with their big cowboy hats, wonderful saggy dirty-white trousers, white linen shirts, and great heavy leather-based belts, nearly a foot extensive, all studded over with brass nails. They wore excessive boots, with their trousers tucked into them, and had lengthy black hair and heavy black mustaches. They are very picturesque, however do now not look prepossessing. On the level they might be set down right away as a few vintage Oriental band of brigands. They are, but, I am knowledgeable, very innocent and instead searching in natural self-declaration.

3)What time did they arrive on the train station?

4)What hats did the Slovaks placed on?

The Meta Guiding (Tracker and Pacer) Method

This refers to one of the maximum set up pace analyzing techniques, which I suspect you're already familiar with after reading via this ebook. Meta-guiding is a simple reading method that entails the usage of an object, e.G., your finger, the cease of a included pen, and so forth., to trace below the fantastic texts you're studying, which act as particular fixation factors ordinary with chunking. Such an item serves as a tracker or pacer in your eyes whilst studying for the duration of written texts.

The number one principle of meta-guiding for pace studying is to move your pacing and tracking item (finger, pen, and so on.) at a tempo that's quicker than your ordinary reading pace. Because the object is supposed to manual your eyes as you have a examine, doing so will pressure your eyes to "capture up" to the quicker than commonplace pace. Over time, your eyes can get used to the quicker tempo, ensuing in a significantly quicker not unusual analyzing pace.

The primary motive why meta-guiding is robust in assisting those who exercise it continuously observe faster is because it minimizes the dependancy of regression. If you do not forget correctly from our earlier communicate, regression is the addiction of going once more to re-have a examine texts you've already observe.

Just to refresh your reminiscence, regression is one of the worst reading conduct someone might also have due to the fact for one, it way that person isn't analyzing properly sufficient to the problem that she or he has to transport decrease again to the textual content just to understand it. And as you recall, going back effectively doubles studying time for the re-have a look at texts and if this occurs frequently, it can bring about sluggish reading velocity. Meta-guiding assist you to beautify your reading speed via making sure which you study each line best as quickly as, which ensures non-forestall development thru the materials you're studying.

Meta guiding is also very clean to exercising! You certainly need your finger to do it!

1)Begin with the useful resource of way of the use of your finger, pen, stylus or some thing contraption to run below precise texts (fixation factors) on the road you're analyzing at a pace that's absolutely slightly quicker than your normal reading pace. Depending in your modern-day chunking capability, it can be 2, 3 or four fixation or prevent factors everyday with line.

2)When you're done with the primary line, have a observe the subsequent thru on foot your tracker or pacer through every of your line's fixation points on the identical speed.

3)Gradually growth the charge at that you float your tracking contraption as you read. Over time, your eyes might be able to have a observe significantly quicker than in recent times.

You can exercise meta-guiding on this newsletter and do not forget, no regression and no sub-vocalizing. Keep your tracker shifting at a everyday pace:

The Wonderful Wizard of Oz — L. Frank Baum
— (624 Words)

Toto got here up, and at once commenced out to bark, however Dorothy made him be however.

The Lion climbed the ladder subsequent, and the Tin Woodman got here last; however each of them cried, "Oh, my!" as quick as they regarded over the wall. When they were all sitting in a row at the pinnacle of the wall, they appeared down and noticed a peculiar sight.

Before them have turn out to be a top notch stretch of u . S . A . Having a ground as clean and shining and white as the lowest of a huge platter. Scattered around were many homes made absolutely of china and painted inside the brightest colorations. These homes were quite small, the maximum essential of them achieving handiest as excessive as Dorothy's waist. There had been additionally quite little barns, with china fences round them; and lots of cows and sheep and horses and pigs and chickens, all manufactured from china, had been repute about in organizations.

But the strangest of all have been the folks that lived on this queer u . S .. There were milkmaids and shepherdesses, with brightly colored bodices and golden spots at some stage in their robes; and princesses with maximum suitable frocks of silver and gold and purple; and shepherds wearing knee breeches with red and yellow and blue stripes down them, and golden buckles on their shoes; and princes with jeweled crowns upon their heads, carrying ermine gowns and satin doublets; and humorous clowns in ruffled robes, with round pink spots upon their cheeks and tall, pointed caps. And, strangest of all, those humans were all made of china, even to their clothes, and were so small that the tallest of them emerge as no higher than Dorothy's knee.

No one did a lot as take a look at the tourists at the begin, besides one little purple china dog with a further-large head, which came to the wall and barked at them in a tiny voice, afterward walking away all another time. "How we could get down?" asked Dorothy.

They positioned the ladder so heavy they couldn't pull it up, so the Scarecrow fell off the wall and the others jumped down upon him in order that the hard ground ought to not hurt their feet. Of course they took pains no longer to mild on his head and get the pins of their toes. When all had been as it need to be down they picked up the Scarecrow, whose frame grow to be quite flattened out, and patted his straw into shape another time.

"We need to bypass this normal area a good way to get to the alternative facet," stated Dorothy, "for it is probably unwise for us to move some other way besides due South."

They started out taking walks via the u . S . Of the china human beings, and the number one issue they came to became a china milkmaid milking a china cow. As they drew near, the cow gave a kick and kicked over the stool, the pail, or maybe the milkmaid herself, and all fell on the china ground with a incredible clatter.

Dorothy was shocked to appearance that the cow had damaged her leg off and that the pail have become mendacity in numerous small portions, while the poor milkmaid had a nick in her left elbow.

"There!" cried the milkmaid angrily. "See what you've got carried out! My cow has damaged her leg, and I have to take her to the mender's save and function it glued on once more. What do you suggest via way of coming proper right here and horrifying my cow?"

"I'm very sorry," all over again Dorothy. "Please forgive us."

But the pretty milkmaid became a exquisite deal too vexed to make any answer. She picked up the leg sulkily and led her cow away, the bad animal limping on three legs. As she left them the milkmaid forged many reproachful glances over her shoulder at the clumsy strangers, preserving her nicked elbow near her side.

The Phrase Reading Technique

This method will allow you to better comprehend what you study, beautify your reading fluency, and make stronger your oral reading abilties. You can also use to enhance your grammar, vocabulary, and punctuation. Here's the manner to perform this method:

Choose Your Reading

Choose the form of reading you want to do, i.E., satisfaction reading or reading to research some element? If you're studying for pleasure, you don't should look at at a quicker clip than important so that you can in reality revel in your reading time. Take the time to understand the material's cadence and rhythms, preference of terms, intellectual imageries, and ideas. Pleasure reading ought to be like pleasure ingesting, i.E., no longer moved quickly.

If you're analyzing to investigate, specially in case you're under ultimate dates, you need to cognizance on understanding the cloth and further importantly, apprehend it within the least quantity of time. You'll want to do velocity analyzing for this kind of analyzing.

Quick Glances

When you begin analyzing, don't stare at phrases but short leaf through phrases. Further, don't even anticipate or say the phrases however give attention to glancing at terms and identifying what they advise. Picture the because of this that of the word as fast as you may in your thoughts.

Again, you want to workout the principle of chunking phrases into terms. Don't take a look at one word at a time.

Imagine or Visualize Every Phrase

This also can take some effort and time within the beginning because of the fact possibilities are, this isn't a few element you're already doing. But do not forget it, studying terms as businesses of letters didn't come certainly to you at the start too. With enough exercising, you can learn how to have a look at with the resource of phrases or word chunks as opposed to in step with word.

Remember, terms are just man or woman symbols that in and with the beneficial resource of themselves hardly ever offers massive mind. It's nice at the same time as phrases are bunched collectively in phrases and sentences that they're capable of specific unique messages. That's why it simplest makes revel in to assume or visualize the because of this of terms rather than character phrases.

Don't Read Too Fast

Yes, tempo reading consists of reading at a significantly quicker charge than ordinary. However, it doesn't imply over-speeding! Just like with the use of, it's possible to over-speed almost about studying.

How do you realize on the identical time as your over-tempo studying? The primary indicator is which you're unable to get the that means of the phrases you're analyzing. Remember, the primary reason of pace reading is to have a look at and recognize more substances within the same length of time. Neither comprehending at a totally gradual tempo nor studying a number of fabric that would't be understood is the essence of pace studying.

When using the word-analyzing method to hurry study, you need as a way to have a take a look at as fast as feasible however despite the fact that being capable of recognize the which means of the phrases you're analyzing. If you focus at the whole on studying phrases faster, comprehension may be compromised. But in case you prioritize analyzing a way to get the that means out of terms, velocity will ultimately have a look at.

This technique is basically the chunking approach but has been laid out barely precise.

You can do that method on the following textual content which has been separated into chunks via one-of-a-kind colors. Read only the gray textual content and allow you to eyes skim over the black: Oliver Twist–Charles Dickens–(601 Words)

For the next eight or ten months, Oliver was the victim of a systematic course of treachery and deception. He was brought up by hand. The hungry and destitute situation of the infant orphan was duly reported by the workhouse authorities to the parish authorities. The parish authorities inquired with dignity of the workhouse authorities, whether there was no female then domiciled in 'the house' who was in a situation to impart to Oliver Twist, the consolation and nourishment of which he stood in need. The workhouse authorities replied with humility that there was not. Upon this, the parish authorities magnanimously and humanely resolved, that Oliver should be 'farmed,' or, in other words, that he should be dispatched to a branch-workhouse some three miles off, where twenty or thirty other juvenile offenders against the poor-laws, rolled about the floor all day, without the inconvenience of too much food or too much clothing, under the parental superintendence of an elderly female, who received the culprits at and for the consideration of seven pence-halfpenny per small head per week. Seven pence-halfpenny's worth per week is a good round diet for a child; a great deal may be got for seven pence-halfpenny, quite enough to overload its stomach and make it uncomfortable. The elderly female was a woman of wisdom and experience; she knew what was good for children; and she had a very accurate perception of what was good for herself. So, she appropriated the greater part of the weekly stipend to her own use and consigned the rising parochial generation to even a shorter allowance than was originally provided for them. Thereby finding in the lowest depth a deeper still; and proving herself a very great experimental philosopher.

Everybody knows the story of another experimental philosopher who had a great theory about a horse being able to live without eating, and who demonstrated it so well, that he had got his own horse down to a straw a day, and would unquestionably have rendered him a very spirited and rampacious animal on nothing at all, if he had not died, four-and-twenty hours before he was to have had his first comfortable bait of air. Unfortunately for, the experimental philosophy of the female to whose protecting care Oliver Twist was delivered over, a similar result usually attended the operation of her system; for at the very moment when the child had contrived to exist upon the smallest possible portion of the weakest possible food, it did perversely happen in eight and a half cases out of ten, either that it sickened from want and cold, or fell into the fire from neglect, or got half-smothered by accident; in any one of which cases, the miserable little being was usually summoned into another world, and there gathered to the fathers it had never known in this.

Occasionally, when there was some more than usually interesting inquest upon a parish child who had been overlooked in turning up a bedstead, or inadvertently scalded to death when there happened to be a washing—though the latter accident was very scarce, anything approaching to a washing being of rare occurrence in the farm—the jury would take it into their heads to ask troublesome questions, or the parishioners would rebelliously affix their signatures to a remonstrance. But these impertinences were speedily checked by the evidence of the surgeon, and the testimony of the beadle; the former of whom had always opened the body and found nothing inside (which was very probable indeed), and the latter of whom invariably swore whatever the parish wanted; which was very self-devotional.

Know What's Best for Your Comprehension

Each person is different. That being said, each person can also benefit differently from different speed reading techniques. If you want to optimize your reading speed, try out one speed reading technique every one or two weeks and record improvements – or lack thereof – in your average reading speed. That's the only way you can objectively determine which technique is best for your reading speed and comprehension.

Chapter 7: Reading Comprehension Tips

I'll never get tired of emphasizing the primary goal of speed reading, which is to optimize reading speed without compromising reading comprehension.   Again,   speed   reading without comprehension is worthless while reading comprehension may not mean much if it takes forever to achieve.

But what does reading comprehension really mean? It refers to the ability to understand what is read. It's an active, intentional, and interactive   endeavor   that   a   person undertakes before, during and after reading a particular material.

With poor reading comprehension, speed reading – or reading for that matter – is nothing more than just looking at and sounding off various symbols. Think of an American who only knows how to read and speak American English trying to read an ancient Chinese scroll from the Ming Dynasty. He may be able to appreciate the aesthetic parts of the scroll's text, but he or she will never be able to really understand what the scroll is saying. For that person, the scroll is meaningless and possibly worthless because all it contains are unintelligible symbols.

More importantly, functional literacy is dependent on good reading comprehension skills. In today's highly competitive world, people need to be able to quickly learn new skills and abilities in order to survive economically. Without adequate reading comprehension skills, it'll be impossible to grow in skills and knowledge and consequently, survive economically.

The SQ3R Method

This is one of the most popular and effective methods for developing reading comprehension. SQ3R stands for:

– S is for Survey;

– Q stands for Question; and

– 3R stands for Read, Recite, and Review.

Here's how to employ the SQ3R method for improving reading comprehension:

Survey

Before reading a chapter or main section of a reading material, survey it first by looking at the following:

1) The title, the main headings and their sub-headings;

2) Any captions provided for maps, charts, graphs, and pictures;

3) Any available study guides or questions;

4) Introducing and concluding paragraphs; and

5) Summaries.

Question

While you're surveying the material, ask questions by, among others:

1) Converting the titles, main headings and subheadings into inquiries or questions;

2) Reading questions at the end of each chapter, main heading or sub-heading, if any are provided; or

3) Asking yourself what you already know about the topic covered by the material.

Read

While you're reading the material:

1) Try to answer the questions you initially raised during the Question portion;

2) If there are any questions provided at the start or end of the chapter or main section, answer them.

3) If there are any captions provided for featured graphics, pictures, charts or tables, read them again;

4) Take note of any words or phrases that were boldfaced, italicized, or underlined for emphasis by the author;

5) When you come across relatively challenging parts, slow down your reading speed;

6) I know I said no regression when reading but for portions of the text that you feel aren't clear, stop and re-read them if you feel they are particularly important; and

Recite

1) Read one section, chapter or paragraph at a time and recite what you understood to be its main points or ideas;

2) Orally summarize the material you read in your own words;

3) After speed reading through the material, re-read and take notes from the material, writing them down in your own words;

4) Highlight or underline the important points you come across with; and

5) Recite!

Review

The review process is fairly simple: just re-speed read your material that's already highlighted with notes taken.

Try this out on an old book you have or a report you wish to understand more thoroughly.

Chapter 8: Calculating Your New Reading Speed

As mentioned earlier, the best way to monitor your speed reading progress is by measuring your actual reading speed, recording them, and comparing your current speed with the previous ones. After giving a particular speed reading technique a try for 7 to 14 days, measure your AS or average reading speed. If you recall, the AS is all about pure reading speed and doesn't check for comprehension. And to remind you how to measure it:

1) Choose a page from a book or a specific reading material.

2) Count the number of words of that page or reading material.

3) Using a timer, record how long it takes you to finish reading your chosen material.

4) Divide the number of words of your chosen reading material by the number of seconds it took you to finish reading it and multiply it by

60 to get your AS, expressed as words-per-minute (WPM).

If you record a higher reading WPM after 7 to 14 days of using a specific technique, it means it's working for you. If you're happy with the progress, you can choose to continue using the technique. If you're not happy with the increase or if your registered new WPM is lower, you can use another technique for another 7 to 14 days and re-measure your reading speed again. And when you do, use this text:

The War of the Worlds–H. G. Wells–(601 Words)

The most extraordinary thing to my mind, of all the strange and wonderful things that happened upon that Friday, was the dovetailing of the commonplace habits of our social order with the first beginnings of the series of events that was to topple that social order headlong. If on Friday night you had taken a pair of compasses and drawn a circle with a radius of five miles around the Woking sand-pits, I doubt if you would have had one human being outside it, unless it were some relation of Stent or of the three or four cyclists or London people lying dead on the common, whose emotions or habits were at all affected by the new-comers. Many people had heard of the cylinder, of course, and talked about it in their leisure, but it certainly did not make the sensation that an ultimatum to Germany would have done.

In London that night poor Henderson's telegram describing the gradual unscrewing of the shot was judged to be a canard, and his evening paper, after wiring for authentication from him and receiving no reply—the man was killed—decided not to print a special edition.

Even within the five-mile circle the great majority of people were inert. I have already described the behavior of the men and women to whom I spoke. All over the district people were dining and supping; working men were gardening after the labors of the day, children were being put to bed, young people were wandering through the lanes love-making, students sat over their books.

Maybe there was a murmur in the village streets, a novel and dominant topic in the public-houses, and here and there a messenger, or even an eye-witness of the later occurrences, caused a whirl of excitement, a shouting, and a running to and fro; but for the most part the daily routine of working, eating, drinking, sleeping, went on as it had done for countless years—as though no planet Mars existed in the sky. Even at Woking station and Horsell and Chobham that was the case.

In Woking junction, until a late hour, trains were stopping and going on, others were shunting on the sidings, passengers were alighting and waiting, and everything was proceeding in the most ordinary way. A boy from the town, trenching on Smith's monopoly, was selling papers with the afternoon's news. The ringing impact of trucks, the sharp whistle of the engines from the junction, mingled with their shouts of "Men from Mars!" Excited men came into the station about nine o'clock with incredible tidings, and caused no more disturbance than drunkards might have done. People rattling Londonwards peered into the darkness outside the carriage windows, and saw only a rare, flickering, vanishing spark dance up from the direction of Horsell, a red glow and a thin veil of smoke driving across the stars, and thought that nothing more serious than a heath fire was happening. It was only around the edge of the common that any disturbance was perceptible. There were half a dozen villas burning on the Woking border. There were lights in all the houses on the common side of the three villages, and the people there kept awake till dawn.

A curious crowd lingered restlessly, people coming and going but the crowd remaining, both on the Chobham and Horsell bridges. One or two adventurous souls, it was afterward found, went into the darkness and crawled quite near the Martians; but they never returned, for now and again a light-ray, like the beam of a warship's searchlight swept the common, and the Heat-Ray was ready to follow.

So, whats your new AS or WPM? Remember, numbers don't lie! That's why measuring or calculating your new reading speed is important for accurately monitoring your speed reading progress.

Chapter 9: External and Internal Reading Optimizers

While speed reading techniques are the primary means by which you can greatly improve the rate at which you read, it doesn't mean it's complete. There are 2 non-reading things you can do that can supplement your speed reading techniques and give you that extra speed reading edge.

These are some more "Captain Obvious" statements here but I had to include them as they really do make a huge difference and it's a good idea to keep them in mind.

Your Reading Environment

If you read in a very noisy or uncomfortable environment, you'll be too distracted to read optimally, regardless of speed. Your reading environment will have a huge impact on your ability to focus on what you're reading and more importantly, on your ability to understand what you're reading.

Some of the most important things you're reading environment must have include:

1) Adequate Lighting: Soft or dim lights can make you feel too relaxed to focus. Too much lighting can also lead to physical discomforts such as eye strain or headaches.

2) Quiet: Even if you're reading in an adequately lit place, a noisy environment will surely distract you or at the very least, prevent you from reading optimally.

3) Privacy: If you're reading in an environment where people can easily disturb you, your chances of being able to focus on your reading is practically zero. That's why unless you live alone or have a room in your house where you can lock yourself to read without being interrupted, it'll be better to go to a well-lit coffee shop or the library instead.

4) The Right Temperature: It'll be hard to concentrate on reading – or any mental endeavor – if you're in an environment that's too hot or too cold. If it's too hot, you'll be sweating like a pig and get dehydrated. If it's too cold, you can feel very sluggish or sleepy and worse, may end up with a major headache.

Chapter 10: What Is Speed Reading?

Do you need to better apprehend the textual content you've got genuinely observe? Do you need to memorize it higher and for an prolonged time? Did you realize you could reap all of your development in half the time spent, in evaluation on your contemporary analyzing pace?

Get acquainted with the expertise of tempo-reading that could offer this, and many different uses.

What is Speed-studying?

There is not any "lengthy-saved thriller" or some aspect like that, but clearly the reality we've got accompanied the incorrect behavior. Find out what tempo-studying is, and discover ways to look at inside the proper, green, and quick manner.

Speed-analyzing is a abilities that allows you to speed up the studying method, growth interest, interest, and memory. The pace studying approach wakes up the capabilities that each person have. They are usually gift, but the problem is that the ones competencies are suffocated in primary faculty. The reading and getting to know techniques we began out to undertake thinking about the reality that number one faculty is inaccurate and hinders us in growing the herbal talents we've.

The intention of pace-studying is like cited above, to rush up reading, but also the analyzing technique. With velocity-analyzing, it's far possible to double the ordinary analyzing pace, and a few also can even triple. While the identical old reading pace is ready 240 terms in line with minute, practiced tempo-readers can without issues check 4 hundred to 800 terms consistent with minute. Speaking of memory, it is demonstrated that tempo-readers memorize round eighty% of the text in a single studying consultation.

History

According to the Psychology Dictionary Online, a tachistoscope is a device which indicates an item, images, numbers, and phrases at the show display. It is also called a T scope. It suggests the devices, numbers, or images a for extremely quick period after which they vanish. These devices have been used for enhancing visible acuity and feature emerge as well-known to check a person's analyzing fee. Pilots in some unspecified time in the destiny of WWII used a tachistoscope to assist them see enemy planes higher and quicker on the identical time as in combat. The tool moreover have become used in the Nineteen Sixties in public colleges as a manner to growth reading pace. These physical video games have been positioned up with every vocabulary and comprehension quizzes.

Evelyn Wood, a researcher, and schoolteacher attempted to understand why some humans read quicker than others. In a second of frustration, she threw down the e-book she have turn out to be reading and left out the pages together together with her hand as she picked it up. She located her hand movement, and that act gave her the concept of the use of a MARKER or a PLACER to have a look at quicker and with greater ordinary overall performance. She advanced the Evelyn Wood's Reading Dynamics in 1959. Historians do not forget this software because the primary speed analyzing direction on the market to the overall public.

As time surpassed, numerous books, one among a kind education techniques that promised studying speeds of up to ten,000+ phrases consistent with mins had been written. Additionally, generation offers myriad online guides and Apps to improve studying pace. The reality is that regardless of which method you operate, except you keep or enhance your reading COMPREHENSION (the potential to interpret and recognize what you've got have a take a look at), then studying speedy is as beneficial as being a performer in a circus sideshow or being a contestant on a skills show.

Basic Methods of Speed Reading

There are 3 desired techniques for reinforcing studying pace. Skimming and scanning, the usage of a pointer/marker, and grouping words collectively/chunking are the 3 favored terms used. Whether you are taking a path in a brick and mortar constructing or online, buy a ebook, or buy an App to observe tempo analyzing, one or greater of the 3 subjects above can be used to illustrate the way to examine quicker.

Why Is Comprehension So Important?

We examine for taken into consideration one of a kind reasons. A fiction reader also can love delving proper into a suspense novel or fantasize about being on the tropical island with a cute companion. Then there can be the pupil of any age, studying to understand a way to do maximum something. Then there may be the reader who desires to discover what the weather may be for the day, what gadgets are on sale at the grocery store's, or what time your grandparents are arriving at the airport. For those who paintings in an place of work placing, the want to study and recognize is paramount. If an administrative assistant gives his/her boss the wrong records, there may be a amazing hazard the job may match to someone else.

Nevertheless, the same is actual for the blue collar worker. If a worker at a manufacturing plant, (allow's use automobiles as an example) didn't observe the memo approximately a exchange in the method of his/her task, tens of millions of greenbacks may be lost due to the mistake made at the equal time as constructing the vehicles.

Moreover, for dad and mom, analyzing to their kids is one in each of their maximum essential roles. For a infant to pay interest language even earlier than she or he might be able to study it, the improvement obtained in mind activity is unsurpassed. If mother or dad doesn't apprehend that the Schoolhouse Rock track, Them Not-so-dry Bones is to be look at or sung with animation and humor, then 3-12 months-antique Mary might be very afraid that there may be a skeleton interior of her body! Furthermore, no longer information or comprehending what dad and mom, kids, unmarried humans, anybody in reality reads, makes studying at 1200 terms in keeping with minute as beneficial as reading at one hundred phrases in line with minute. Comprehension is the vital thing to analyzing.

Chapter 11: What Are the Benefits to Improving Reading Speed?

The most apparent advantage to analyzing faster is to keep time. However, before identifying how a fantastic deal greater net surfing, snoozing, workout, or some component other assignment being a brief reader will add mins to, you want to remember the 5 W's: Who are you reading for? What fabric are you analyzing? When are you studying the text? Where are you reading it? And, most significantly, why are you analyzing inside the first area?

Who?

If you are a pupil who loves mathematics, studying Shakespeare may be greater daunting to you than a student who studies a language. If you are an employee of an coverage commercial enterprise employer, you can need to re-read the present day-day suggestions issued with the beneficial aid of the government greater than once so you can supply an reason in the back of the information to your clients. If you want to deliver a hand-written letter on your boy/girl buddy, you in reality need to ensure the phrases are spelled and used correctly. For instance: Will you receive my concept? May be very unique than Will you anticipate my idea? Understanding what you are studying is going hand in hand with what you're writing, so earlier than you tell your consumer that the new regulation manner this, or ask your boy/lady buddy if you could take to the dance, make certain you understand your target audience and recognize that what you are saying is interpreted successfully.

What?

What shape of text you are analyzing, how lengthy it is, and what is its motive determines the velocity at which you need to study. For instance, in case you are analyzing fabric with sudden vocabulary, analyzing it cautiously is particularly important. Later in this e-book, we'll talk the SQ3R reading approach, which need for use each time you examine an extraordinary or complicated textual content.

When?

Are you a morning individual, or do you pick an all-nighter to check for an examination? Learn while your thoughts functions at its top notch. Any technical or atypical text must be have a look at on the same time as you are at your maximum alert. Many humans take a look at fiction or specific fun studying material in advance than mattress. For most of them, the act is to relax, permit the interest inside the mind settle, and doze off. That's not the time to look at your company's marketing strategy or look at for a statistics test. When the thoughts is at its exquisite, you may train your eyes to look the net web page in a special manner; this is the essence of pace reading. It takes an entire lot of exercising, and it is a skills to be used whilst you're at your excellent.

Where?

Many human beings revel in that they have a look at quality whilst there may be music or information noise. Studies have validated that loud, top 40's song (which adjustments with each generation) has a big horrible effect on comprehension with both university college students and adults. Some research have tested that even historic beyond noise including the hum of an air-conditioner, or the hissing of a radiator are counter-green to comprehension. On the alternative hand, classical song has been used effectively to growth interest and focus for readers. Conversely, for personnel who are doing the same venture all day (bear in mind our car employee?), any music playing constantly in the historical past permits them to recognition on an person undertaking as opposed to doing the identical hassle again and again. In cease, in case you anticipate having your headphones on permits you look at and understand higher, it doesn't. You need to be in a fairly quiet vicinity to study for information, even though the "information" is a chunk of writing approximately planting corn or a romance novel set in Paris. You will pass over a part of the author's intentions; that's no longer a disaster while analyzing for delight, however can result in a sequence of unlucky activities if you are distracted whilst analyzing a few trouble essential.

Why?

If you observed you understand why numerous your analyzing tempo is critical, you then understood the number one 4 W's: who, what, while, and in which. Here is a quick lesson for you concerning your studying degree. Try to reply the questions without looking at the textual content above. Answers is probably furnished on the end of this economic disaster.

1.When analyzing, you have to generally have a few exciting tune gambling?

TRUE

FALSE

2.The top notch way to recognize what you're studying is usually to examine it instances.

TRUE

FALSE

three.Being a notable-rapid reader will help you write better?

TRUE

FALSE

four.You need to continuously entire technical or complex analyzing in the course of the day.

TRUE

FALSE

five. What you are studying must determine the velocity of which you are reading.

TRUE

FALSE

Once you apprehend your analyzing dreams and functions, then you may start to exercise velocity analyzing. This ebook will communicate all 3: skimming/scanning, the pointer/marker, or grouping/chunking. Most importantly, it'll usually consciousness on retaining or improving comprehension. The want for speed doesn't outweigh the want to understand.

All of the solutions are FALSE, except for range five, it sincerely is correct.

Chapter 12: What Are the Techniques for Speed Reading?

Skimming and Scanning

Most readers have used skimming and scanning of their daily lives. Skimming is the exercising of reviewing textual content thru studying excessive exceptional factors of a non-fiction textual content with the idea of identifying what material desires to be study. Scanning isn't always analyzing the least bit. It is the usage of your eyes to discover the precise piece of facts for that you had been searching. Using a marker or your finger enables whilst scanning for information. Scanning is used to find dates, a cellphone amount or cope with, or a specific name, for example.

Both of those strategies will in fact boom your reading tempo. For one element, you aren't studying at all while you check. You are searching terms for a selected word or variety. The assignment of scanning can be practiced using gadgets, a deck of playing cards, an series of swatches of material; having a set of some factor and being requested to find out a specific object is scanning on the equal time as searching on the textual content. Additionally, there is not a remarkable deal statistics of the because of this of the textual content from skimming it or scanning it; therefore, the cause of learning from what you are analyzing will become a moot detail. There is, but, an effective manner to observe the phrases you want to look at to determine which elements you may want to popularity on more cautiously. Let's name that surveying.

A land surveyor appears through a tool to measure distance, elevation, and distinctive important features of vicinity earlier than developing a blueprint for the building at the manner to occupy that land. Surveying text earlier than you study it's miles very similar. You diploma what you want to take a look at intensive, what the subject of every paragraph is, what's vital records indoors a certain paragraph, after which growing your blueprint for reading the material.

Skimming

•Read the number one sentence of each paragraph;

•Read the very last sentence of each paragraph

•Read key phrases inner every paragraph

Scanning

•Visualize what you are trying to find – see the phrase you're searching out

Use seen clues inside the text

o Capital letters

o Italics

o Boldface

•Use a systematic scanning sample...run your eyes down the center of the column of textual content and zig zag from side to side to discover your phrase

Surveying

•Read the name

•Read the primary paragraph

•Read all headings, italicized/boldfaced terms, graphs, charts and tables

•Read the final paragraph

Let's use a monetary spoil in a history e-book as an example. If you skim it, you continue to need to go through the whole bankruptcy yet again, studying the paragraphs you decided what may be vital. If you scanned the monetary catastrophe, then you definitely didn't study for any statistics. You may additionally have a have a take a look at guide from your instructor and positioned simplest the specific data required for the exam. That is excellent whilst the purpose is to earn an top notch score; but, if you want to have a have a look at what the chapter changed into approximately, scanning received't do hundreds. There isn't any comprehending through scanning. Skimming most effective offers you with the land surveyor's blueprints. Unless you bypass back and re-study what you highlighted, now not a few component will ever be built, blueprints or now not. Skimming has its cause...reviewing for an exam is one correct instance; to that cease, don't suppose that the utilization of every method can be all you need to do to increase your analyzing tempo as a way to decorate your analyzing. There isn't always any comprehension; therefore, little might be retained.

Surveying cloth for data is extra green. You are reading the primary and last sentence of every paragraph, and looking for key phrases in among. Unless the report makes use of a number of complicated and prolonged sentences, then surveying is analyzing the entire fabric besides. How does that increase studying pace? It may not double your fee, but it'll decorate your know-how of the material because you're skipping the a great deal much less vital sentences in every paragraph but even though getting the gist of the which means. Rate can also continue to be approximately the same, however there's no re-studying (skimming) and you've examine the cloth with a totally particular set of suggestions. Your blueprints have made developing the structure less complex and with a incredible statistics of what to do. Translate that during your lifestyles: that's an terrific mark on the check, a vending inside the place of business, or a 15% boom in income to your industrial business enterprise. That's a exquisite manner to observe and look at the information.

Using a Marker

A marker or a pointer can be your finger, a pen or pencil, or any type of stick. The motive of the tool is to train your eyes to appearance terms no longer as person objects at the internet web page, however as an possibility as a group of gadgets that make feel.

Evelyn Wood, who coined the time period "speed studying" evolved a application referred to as Reading Dynamics, which have turn out to be a a hit software program application used to enhance analyzing velocity. It's said that US presidents John F. Kennedy, Jimmy Carter, and Gerald Ford took the seven-day path to help them with the big amount of information they needed to observe on a each day basis. There is a story that John F. Kennedy ought to have a have a look at the complete New York Times newspaper in 10 minutes! Critics (and realists) claim that considering he had already been briefed on the times' current activities, all he became doing changed into scanning the paper, no longer analyzing it. Regardless, he did lease pace studying strategies to decorate his analyzing tempo.

Most international locations look at from left to right; but, in case your language is take a look at from right to left, truely contrary the carrying activities concerning the use of a marker to beautify tempo. The pointer method is a education exercised this is designed to permit a reader to peer the entire web page of a e-book as a whole, studying vertically in place of horizontally. Therefore, the method works for every left to right and proper to left studying.

Many children have been taught to examine the use of the pointer approach. Often, the teacher ought to bypass his/her finger throughout the web page as the student have a look at each word. By grade 3 or 4, university university students had been trained to "finger have a look at" on their personal. The advantage have come to be to permit the scholar to live centered, study the first-rate quantity of recent vocabulary that number one university brings to a person's brain, and to assist them understand every phrase for themselves.

, to call some. This part of the language is for absolutely everyone, now not the designers of pc applications, hardware, and Apps. Therefore, we, too, as person readers come upon new language each day.☐As adults, we although encounter new vocabulary. Because of era, we've got had to have a study a new set of vocabulary: texting, emails, cursor, cloud-based totally definitely actually, dropbox, emoji

The pointer approach (there are carrying sports activities in chapter 4) allows a reader to learn how to see a set of phrases on a line and device them as one perception. That will growth speed, honestly. The way to hold the comprehension intact is to understand the which means of the group, in area of the person terms. It takes time and exercising, and the results may be exceptional.

Chunking

The excellent way to discover ways to "bite" is with the resource of manner of using the pointer approach. The reason of getting to know to chunk phrases into organizations of , three, four, or even five is to decorate your reading charge. In order to do that, a whole lot of exercising is critical, and seeking out to bypass over the start steps won't artwork. It may additionally additionally take you five weeks to apply the method with out a marker for almost all of the studying you do. Remember: the charge at which you read desires to vary based on the type of text you're analyzing. If you need to increase your analyzing rate all spherical, even if the textual content is new or greater complicated, then you may want to comply with the steps and workout wearing activities in financial ruin 4 AND continuously workout them till they end up the simplest technique you operate to examine.

Chapter 13: Practice Exercises

There isn't always any ONE piece of textual content to use to exercising analyzing strategies. This financial ruin will come up with the pointers and some pattern excerpts to look and find out how the method works. However, to great decorate your reading tempo, use cloth this is relevant to your analyzing wishes: non-fiction, fiction, textbooks, magazines, newspapers, organization plans, a letter (an email counts) from a loved one...the list is limitless, and your practice texts SHOULD variety. The quit cause is to take a look at faster on the equal time as maintaining and/or developing comprehension. To accumulate this, you need to look at the techniques for precise kinds of substances.

Choosing Your Practice Pieces

Just like a musician makes use of numerous rankings to workout, you moreover mght need to differ your workout quantities. Remember: the song a amateur uses is considered one in all a type than a member of a symphony orchestra...select tough quantities that are thrilling to you and embody records approximately that you are quite acquainted.

A government first rate also can experience information, a e-book written through a leader of his/her us of a, a completely unique with a ancient attitude, a recent idea concerning new tool purchases, and the the the front internet page of the newspaper as his/her picks. On the other hand, a primary university teacher also can select out a textbook about behavior manage inside the school room, a completely unique approximately a summer time romance, the contemporary e-e-newsletter from the college, and the sports sports segment of the newspaper. The component right here is to pick material this is extended sufficient so that you could have a take a look at exclusive picks whilst you workout and feature super genres of textual content to select from, mainly if your goal is to be an ordinary quicker reader.

Skimming/Scanning/Surveying

Although the ones techniques won't boom the price and improve comprehension on their private, mastering the way to skim, check and survey are beneficial and useful for certain varieties of reading.

Exercise 1: Skimming for Understanding

Directions: Read the primary line and the very last line of every stanza (equal as a paragraph in textual content), then look for key terms within every stanza. The purpose ought to be to recognize the meaning of the song even as now not having heard it or having test each word.

In silence, an eagle soars,

as vapors convey him higher,

through darkish horizons.

It isn't fearful of its scorn,

because of the reality the typhoon's temperament

best offers him greater power.

With worry, comes courage,

in adversity, the evolution of the individual.

An eagle turns into an eagle,

best whilst it has observed out to cope with a storm.

In the geographical areas of pain,

while every heartbeat

bleeds speechless tears,

whilst phrases are suffocated,

submerging you into uncharted waters;

pay attention - for every ache and struggling

is the provenance of expertise.

With suffering, empathy is born.

What did you understand after analyzing? Initially, hard to understand the which means, however you could development every subsequent time. If you look at ONLY the number one and closing line of every stanza we will apprehend that overcoming the troubles and adversity makes us stronger.

Exercise 2: Skimming Text

Try all over again to skim the subsequent cloth. Read the primary line, the remaining line of each paragraph and search for any key terms interior. Then try to answer the questions on the stop of the exercise. This is a letter of advice for a secondary arithmetic instructor.

Dear Selection Committee:

As a pro educator, I've written many letters of advice through the years. Writing this letter on behalf of Sedrick Kennedy brings every delight and remorse. He, by means of manner of manner of a long way, is the most exceptional educator and colleague with whom I've had the pleasure to art work in my 20+ years of coaching.

Mr. Kennedy has mastered the competencies required to train secondary arithmetic in any respect tiers. As a fellow Advanced Placement educator for the Bainbridge Island School District, I absolutely have witnessed his strength of mind, perseverance, and steady desire to prepare his students for the AP Calculus Exam every May. Moreover, he has succeeded at the usage of those equal abilities to teach regular degree Algebra 2 and geometry university college students, which normally includes a great-primarily based absolutely, severa pupil populace, from the most decided to the least interested of inexperienced persons.

Mr. Kennedy's person, coupled collectively along with his schooling and revel in, permit him to create and make bigger each of his training to end up its very personal private analyzing community. He spends the number one severa weeks of the twelve months looking and listening, then makes use of his uncanny functionality to apprehend each student as an character, and starts offevolved offevolved to train the route to a hard and fast of college students, who, via the surrender of the three hundred and sixty five days, have turn out to be a collective who paintings together, ask questions, undertaking every one-of-a-kind, and, most importantly, are a circle of relatives. What amazes me is that each class has a selected disposition, and Sedrick manages to provide every pupil the fine viable instructional revel in this is every fun and tough. He has had a 100% passing price at the AP Calculus Exam for the past 5 years and has had the same fulfillment charge collectively collectively together with his End of Course assessments.

Mr. Kennedy's fulfillment is done no longer with the useful aid of training the concern rely; as an opportunity, his college college students are supplied with the strategies and abilties that enabled them to have a take a look at and keep the hassle bear in mind. Our school rooms are component thru manner of aspect, and the powerful energy and discovery he brings to his college students seem to permeate through the walls. He has showed himself as an educator in the lecture room, much like the weight room supervisor (training right approach further to how to amplify the frame for a particular exercising), and has been an crucial part of the immoderate college's Diversity Council for severa years.

As a colleague, Sedrick is a part of the group and has helped our branch to come to be a more synchronous and collaborative organization with the purpose of providing a fine analyzing surroundings for each student within the faculty. He is high-quality to artwork with, constantly takes the time to answer questions from his fellow instructors, parents, and the management. He goes above and past the query, regularly gaining knowledge of and sharing more than grow to be requested. He is a first-rate buddy and a welcome aid both professionally and individually.

I quite propose Sedrick Kennedy as a member of the teaching frame of humans at Your Secondary School. He will honestly be a first rate addition in your mathematics branch. Please feel unfastened to contact me if you have any questions.

Regards,

Delany Maritz

Mathematics Department

My Secondary School

Now, do no longer look once more on the story. Based off your SKIMMING the letter, try and solution the subsequent questions:

1. This is a letter written via a colleague.

TRUE

FALSE

2. The letter is ready a male.

TRUE

FALSE

3.The person the letter is ready teaches mathematics.

TRUE

FALSE

4.The individual writing the letter has been coaching for many years.

TRUE

FALSE

5. You can inform that the character had been given the approach with the aid of reading this letter?

TRUE

FALSE

If you skimmed the letter, you want to are becoming the solutions correct. The answers are all real; however, YOUR option to extensive variety 5 want to be FALSE. You cannot understand by using using studying a letter of recommendation whether or not or no longer the person had been given the location or now not.

Exercise 3: Surveying to Understand Text

Let's pass scanning for a 2d. Remember, surveying requires some studying. Look on the become aware of of the chapter, READ the primary and closing paragraph, search for any italicized or boldface terms or headings. Since the Freud piece is exceptional 4 paragraphs from the entire chapter, there aren't any subtitles or other top notch stand-outs in the excerpt. Still, flow in advance and SURVEY the Freud choice. Answer the questions again. Did any of your solutions trade because you had extra facts?

If you consider the 2 sporting events you in reality finished, ask your self if one t considerably extra time than the opposite. Chances are they did now not. Additionally, did you advantage greater information (comprehension) from skimming or from surveying? Skimming serves its motive to decide what you can, as a reader, need to greater critically have a look at in some time. Surveying, if completed efficiently, need to reply the bulk of your questions at the same time as no longer having to move lower decrease back to re-have a observe for data.

Both of those techniques are designed to assist absolutely everyone be a better reader. They every may even increase your velocity IF they'll be completed correctly, used for the ideal motive, and practiced again and again. THINK approximately the five W's earlier than you make a decision which approach to apply to study a few factor.

Exercise 4: Scanning to Find an Object

Scanning isn't studying. It's searching out a selected "some factor" as speedy as you can. There is a deck of playing gambling playing cards on the subsequent web page. Set a timer earlier than you have a have a look at them and word how prolonged it takes you to discover the ten of spades.

Did you find it? (10th card from the left). Even despite the fact that most of the spade (♠) is included, when you have used a deck of cards, you understand that there are black fits and the 10 of clubs is in truth seen. Thus, the 10 of spades is the next card. Scanning requires some vital set of competencies; a extraordinary purpose why we love infants to play with blocks, Legos, and specific tactile toys that teach them the manner to check for excellent matters ("Find the blue block.")

Exercise 5: Scanning for Information

Okay, now allow's attempt the same exercise using phrases. Remember to time yourself.

On the subsequent internet net web page is a technique description taken from the net hobby postings in The Cleveland Plain Dealer. See how lengthy it takes to:

1.Determine if the hobby is a part-time or entire-time

2.Determine what stage of schooling is needed for the location.

three. Determine the income for the task.

Time every are searching for for my part. Scanning is typically for one particular object.

Ready? Go!

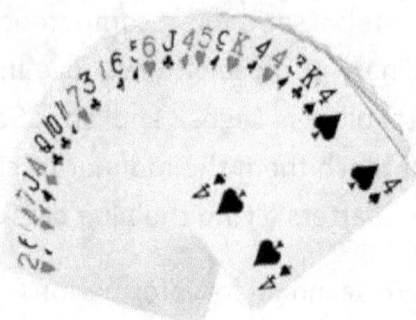

Did you find out all three answers? If you likely did, then you definately have real skills and don't need to analyze tempo analyzing strategies: there may be no profits posted in the ad. Trick query. Here's why that exercise become given: teachers, HR managers, machine recruiters often have university university college students and applicants take a check for employment. One of the devices can be similar to the question about the income for the job posting you checked out. Most recruiters are looking for to determine your functionality to noticeably have a look at a scenario or hassle that can be a part of the procedure. If you are scanning ONLY for the solutions, and there can be a trick query, you will likely find out yourself out of the taking walks due to the truth you didn't look at for the motive supposed.

Using a Marker and Chunking

You can select out what shape of marker or pointer works splendid for you. A finger, a pen or pencil, a chopstick are all suitable selections to start. The intention of using a marker is to start "chunking" phrases into , three, four, and further companies. Therefore, the marker exercising is probably a stepping stone to begin reading a way to chunk. As stated in advance, accomplishing the capability of chunking terms into businesses at the same time as preserving your information of the information is what tempo reading is. The motive is to chew without using a marker.

The following physical video games if you need to exercise chunking. For each exercising, time your self. The variety of phrases in each desire is probably in parentheses at the end. Divide the range of terms inside the desire by the point it took to examine. That will offer you with a everyday with minute analyzing rate.

For the primary exercising, examine along with your marker moving at some point of the net net page over every phrase. This need to give you a studying pace this is very much like your regular studying price due to the reality there can be no chunking of phrases. Typically, an person reads among hundred-three hundred phrases constant with minute. Keep in mind, in case your fee is 100 WPM or four hundred WPM, chunking need to help growth that huge variety, thereby developing your tempo and saving you time on the identical time as analyzing.

Exercise 6: Reading with a Marker Word through Word

Halloween Tricks

October thirty first is known as Halloween, All Hallows' Eve, or Trick or Treat in masses of components of the area. I am from a small island close to Seattle, Washington in the United States. For my three kids, knocking on doors and getting candy become what Halloween come to be all about. Until ultimate 365 days, that is.

My 16-12 months-antique son had a date, and my 13-year-antique daughter and eleven-12 months-antique son have been every invited to activities; reputedly, the following degree within the birthday party of spookiness and fun. I had the satisfaction of being the "discern driver" that night time, and come to be tasked with selecting up my son at nine:00 pm and my daughter at 9:30. It all appeared perfectly choreographed.

I had three hours to spend on my own...an uncommon occurrence. So, I determined to have my Halloween deal with and get a spa treatment. I went to the salon and come to be prepared to be pampered; however, they had been closing early for the "excursion," and all they'd time for have end up a facial. Oh properly, at the least I'll have half-hour of peace, I belief as Myrna took me lower lower back to a small room that smelled of lavender. There were lit candles and small LED lights to create a calming temper. I met Holly, who might be giving me my facial. She seemed very terrific, and as she had me sit down in a heated, notably clean reclining chair, she made a shaggy dog story and snorted while she laughed!

The subsequent half-hour have been not very enjoyable. Holly gave me a exquisite facial; but, she talked the entire time. She laughed and snorted hundreds I had a chunk of a headache by the time she turn out to be completed. So plenty for me time. What to do subsequent?

The island is instead rural, and the wood are vintage and moss-covered. I determined to be realistic and take a trial pressure to find out the residence where my son modified into having his party. I knew wherein my daughter modified into, but Liam, my son, changed into at the south surrender of the island, on a avenue that wasn't maintained via the metropolis. That meant that there may be a whole lot of little children on foot round for trick or treat and there might possibly be a bit moderate. So, I programmed my iPhone and accompanied the instructions. I stopped at Starbucks for a Caramel Macchiato at the manner, determining to loosen up in my car and take note of music. I grow to be determined to have some me time. (410)

Exercise 8: Read with a Marker THREE WORD CHUNKING

For this exercising, you may separate the phrases yourself into three-word chunks in case you'd like. You need to first try and look at with out distinction, even though, because of the reality you within the suggest time are schooling at a degree that ought to suggest an boom to your price, but and not using a assist isolating the phrases besides with the very important marker and your eyes seeing three phrases at a time.

The guy walked spherical my automobile, stopped at my window and checked out me with subject. I concept that probable I had facial cream left over on my nostril due to the truth he seemed perplexed. "Can you placed it in a park and pull up the emergency brake?"

"No hassle," I responded and did what he requested. I must feel the auto transferring backwards slowly, and I saved fearing that I have become knocking over lawn decorations or very high-priced shrubs. "It keeps moving besides I hold my foot on the brake."

"Are you able to do this? I think you need to."

"No hassle. This is what I get for in search of to loosen up at the same time as my kids are at their occasions this night. My call is Sarah. Thanks for preventing."

"I'm John," the person stated. "I expect we're going to need a winch to pull you out of here.

Let me see if the Livingston's have get right of entry to to at the least one, and attempt to determine a way to get you out of here." He walked down the driveway wherein my car modified into a short time in advance than. I saw the individual of the residence stroll towards John and the two have been talking.

In the meantime, I'm below the influence of alcohol my Caramel Macchiato and texted my husband to tell him I modified into in a ditch. We hadn't seen each extraordinary the least bit that day, and I was hoping he'd say he'll bring his truck and pull me out. He responded to my text with a question or approximately how I even have come to be; but, he didn't offer any assist. That emerge as peculiar, but I didn't absolutely care that plenty. How tough is it going to be to get my vehicle driven beforehand and again on the road?

John and Steve Livingston came once more to the window of my vehicle. "How are you doing? Did you damage your self?"

"Um, no, I'm wonderful. I want I didn't reduce to rubble your landscaping , and that's all."

"I suppose we are going to want to call a tow truck to pull you out of proper here. I don't see how a pickup can do it. How's your foot at the destroy?"

"You recognize, it's uncommon due to the fact I definitely have Multiple Sclerosis, and I pressure with feet because of the truth my proper foot is inclined. So. I've were given my left foot without troubles on the brake, my Starbucks, and my cell cellphone. I'm high-quality. Really, I am. I count on I'll name a few towing agencies and be aware who can get proper right here the quickest. My foot is best now, but I do now not assume I want to try this for too lengthy."

"Good idea. Is there something you need whilst you are equipped?" (438)

Exercise nine: Read with a Marker FOUR WORD CHUNKING

00004.JpegNow the rate of your analyzing need to be at least double that of your word with the resource of word studying. The passage might be pink and black print first, then all black print 2nd. USE YOUR MARKER. At this issue, you need to begin to see the net page VERTICALLY in preference to HORIZONTALLY. In super phrases,

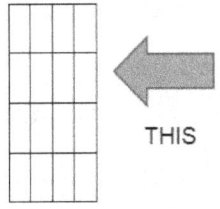

THIS

As you notice companies of phrases, your eyes are being knowledgeable to peer the internet web page as an entire image, breaking it up into smaller pics. Remember to set your timer.

I shook my head and requested Siri to find me the nearest towing enterprise. I determined some thing new that night. There are four unique cellular telephone numbers for towing that carrier the island, and they all belonged to the equal business enterprise. After 20 minutes or so, I heard decrease again from the dispatcher and may must wait as a minimum an hour. Great, I concept. It changed into 7:15 and I nevertheless failed to understand in which my son have turn out to be, and I needed to be there thru 9:00 pm. Keep calm, Sarah, you can make it.

John and Steve saw that I became off the cellphone and walked again to my opened window. "Did you locate someone to pop out?" John asked.

"Yes, but it will likely be at least an hour. Apparently, tow truck drivers need to celebration on Halloween." I laughed and noticed that neither gentleman joined me. I idea it became a bit funny.

Then Steve said, "Sarah, I anticipate we ought to call the hearth branch to sturdy your automobile and get you out of there. You are creeping backwards a touch more."

"Oh, I'll be first-class. It's a loopy night time time at the island. I do no longer need to hassle the fireplace department!"

"Trust us. We want to get your car stable and get you out of there. And the second one you take your foot off the brake, the auto is going to move masses quicker."

"Okay, then. Do you mind putting round till they get proper right here? I'm shape of embarrassed." I clearly felt like they had been treating me like a helpless female who couldn't get herself out of the dust. But I have become grateful that they've been there as it become darkish, bloodless, and rain changed into now coming down.

I texted my husband once more to tell him what grow to be going on. He called me to look how I turned into. He have become at his mother's residence, approximately forty five mins away, so regardless of the truth that I was hoping he'd come to assist, I knew a pick out-up wasn't going to do it.

135

"I didn't assume a select out-up could probably do it, hon. It looks as if you're honestly stuck. What's round you?"

"Well, there may be a large tree subsequent to my door, so I'm going to want to transport slowly out the passenger aspect. That issue appears quite easy. I'm simply satisfied I did now not run over his landscaping. It's so embarrassing."

"Well, hold in there, and textual content me at the same time as you are out. Do they apprehend you've got got were given MS?"

"Yes. I need to be adequate if I can walk on the alternative factor of the car."

"Well, prevent your Starbucks and hold close in there. At least help is on the way." (441)

Same passage USE YOUR MARKER FOR FOUR WORDS AT A TIME

I shook my head no and asked Siri to discover me the nearest towing service. I found something new that nighttime. There are 4 one-of-a-kind phone numbers for towing that provider the island, however all of them belonged to the identical organization. After 20 minutes or so, I heard yet again from the dispatcher and will have to wait at the least an hour. Great, I belief. It end up 7:15 and I nonetheless did now not recognize in which my son became, and I needed to be there by means of manner of 9:00 pm. Keep calm, Sarah, you can make it.

John and Steve located that I turned into off the phone and walked again to my opened window. "Did you find someone to pop out?" John requested.

"Yes, but it is going to be at the least an hour. Apparently, tow truck drivers need to party on Halloween." I laughed and noticed that neither gentleman joined me. I concept it turned into a touch funny.

Then Steve stated, "Sarah, I assume we ought to name the hearth branch to steady your automobile and get you out of there. You are creepy backwards a chunk greater."

"Oh, I'll be exceptional. It's a crazy night time on the island. I do not need to bother the fireplace branch!"

"Trust us. We want to get your automobile constant and get you out of there. And the second you are taking your foot off the brake, the auto goes to transport plenty faster."

"Okay, then. Do you thoughts striking round until they get proper here? I'm form of embarrassed." I genuinely felt like they were treating me like a helpless female who couldn't get herself out of the dust. But I was grateful that they have been there because it grow to be dark, bloodless, and rain have become now coming down.

I texted my husband another time to tell him what emerge as taking place. He called me to appearance how I became. He modified into at his mom's residence, about forty five minutes away, so even though I hoped he'd come to assist, I knew a pick out-up wasn't going to do it.

"I failed to expect a select-up ought to do it, hon. It looks like you are in truth caught. What's round you?"

"Well, there may be a large tree next to my door, so I'm going to need to move slowly out the passenger aspect. That side appears quite clear. I'm just glad I did no longer run over his landscaping. It's so embarrassing."

"Well, draw close in there, and text me at the same time as you're out. Do they recognise you have got MS?"

"Yes. I want to be k if I can walk at the possibility factor of the car."

"Well, end your Starbucks and draw close in there. At least help is on the manner." (441)

Now you have have been given been tempo reading. What if your price is similar to at the same time as you have a look at one word at a time; regardless of a marker? Simple, keep working towards. Follow these hints and recommendations:

•Use your studying material.

•Practice with paintings chunking until you enjoy your eyes seeing the phrases at a time

•Move to a few then 4-word chunking at the same time as your eyes and thoughts inform you they may be prepared

•Practice at least 15 minutes a day WHEN YOU ARE AT YOUR BEST

•Do no longer get discouraged if reading faster takes some time. You are changing the manner your mind interprets what it's far seeing

•Practice comprehension. Find studying selections that have quizzes or questions collectively with them so you may be sure you recognize what you look at. You can ask a person to jot down a few questions for you, purchase a have a have a study guide for the e book, or look on-line. There is a tremendous threat you'll find out techniques to check your self on what you're studying.

The the relaxation the exercising physical video games are the relaxation of the Halloween Tricks story. The phrase rely variety for every choice is at the forestall. Additionally, there are comprehension questions regarding the whole story. They are in no unique order, so looking to answer them without reading the rest of the monetary disaster may also display difficult.

Exercise 10

So, I did what he cautioned. I observed a few "trick or treaters" who determined my vehicle but failed to appear too concerned. There had been now about a 1/2 of dozen buddies popularity at the Livingston's porch, looking ahead to the fireplace department and searching out to live dry.

About ten minutes later, I see exceptional red flashing lighting and concentrate a short beep from the very big fireside engine using cautiously in the route of me. There had been 3 firemen, complete with their tools on, jumping down from the truck walking to me.

"Are you injured, Ma'am? What took place? Do you want medical institution remedy?" The senior fireman, Hank, listened at the same time as I informed him what befell. He suggested his crew to set up a perimeter, block off the street, and get a chain to wrap round a tree throughout the street. Everything turned into taking vicinity so speedy. They appeared even more worried than the pals. I modified into nonetheless stressed with the aid of using their behavior; however, I modified into equipped to get out of the automobile.

Hank asked me to roll down the window on the passenger thing. He described everything his guys were doing to stable my automobile to the tree so it would not skip after I took my foot off the brake. A policeman in his patrol automobile showed up because the firemen have been roping off the vicinity and getting my car hooked to the chain. A gentleman stopped in which the firemen had positioned caution tape to close the street. I did now not see that avenue in advance. I'll bet that's wherein Liam is. At least I had a quite pinnacle risk of selecting him up on time.

"You recognize there is no one-of-a-kind way out of right right right here," the gentleman stated to the fireside chief.

"I'm sorry sir. We have a scenario that is a precedence."

"Okay. I bet I'll surely skip again to the party." He had been given in his car and drove in contrary. I could not see wherein he went due to the fact the street sloped downward. (323)

Exercise eleven

"Okay, Sarah. Are you prepared to take your foot off the brake? I nodded positive. "Do it slowly, please."

I felt the automobile jerk backwards and stopped midway from taking my foot off certainly.

"It's k. I promise you your car may not keep shifting. Go beforehand and release the brake."

I did. I felt the initial jerk from the wheels of my automobile now not having the brakes on anymore, but Hank changed into proper and I even have come to be steady. Yeah! I get out of here! I modified into prepared to transport now.

I genuinely have located out to look my MS as more of a nuisance than a disability, and I honestly have not permit it save you me from residing my existence. I stroll with a recommended limp on my right side, and while Hank determined me use my arms to beautify my leg over the middle console of my vehicle to get to the passenger facet, I determined the priority on his face. I've lived with that for 30 years and generally provide an purpose at the back of that it appears worse than it's miles.

Before I had a threat to say something, Hank had his group lay a long ladder down on the comb, had them assist me out-out the car, and the three of them helped me stroll on each rung of the ladder till I turn out to be efficiently at the pavement. As that is taking place, I'm questioning that now I'm performing similar to the helpless woman who desires rescued. I emerge as so embarrassed.

The lighting from the fire engine have been shining brightly on my car. When I in the end controlled to show and look at it, I knew why anybody saved asking if I emerge as adequate. My automobile become across the road, not subsequent to it, from the Livingston's house, the front wheels within the air, about 15 feet in a ravine that dropped off about 30 feet. It took me a few minutes to realise how fortunate I actually have end up to have the assist I did and expressed my appreciation to all. (331)

Exercise 12

My Halloween trick wasn't quite over but. I sat in the once more of a police automobile for forty five mins looking for the tow truck. Officer Geary have become great and saved me company whilst I waited. The chief of police lives in the community, and his daughter added us a few sweet, so the night time time time wasn't all terrible!

I had about 10 mins to spare in advance than I needed to pick up Liam. Sure sufficient, the third house down that extremely tough to see "street" become wherein he have become. I parked inside the driveway and waited. Liam and his friend, Ari, had been given within the automobile and started out their monolog of the night time time's festivities. I drove slowly and carefully, silently thanking God that I had my exceptional children, and we have been collectively.

"...then a few man got here to the door and said the street turn out to be closed cuz someone have been given stuck in a ditch. The hearth department and police might not permit each person through. Did you have got were given got any problems, Mom?" asked my precious son.

" Not the least bit, sweetheart. I cushty for hours."

Epilogue

It seems that the big surprise of the night was that my husband traded in his truck for a new pricey sedan; a Halloween address for the circle of relatives. I think my nighttime in a ditch wasn't so awful in any case. Unfortunately, I nonetheless am no longer prison to pressure the ultra-cutting-edge automobile! (229)

Comprehension Questions Halloween Tricks

1.The most crucial man or woman, Sarah, is a?

A. Teenager

B. Grandmother

C. Mother

D. Father

2.Sarah is in her vehicle due to the truth

A, she needed to get groceries

B. She needed to pick out out up her youngsters

C. She modified into the usage of to her mom's house

D. She didn't need her own family to appearance her ingesting candy

3.What "excursion" is being celebrated?

A.Christmas

B.Chinese New Year

C.Halloween

D. Cinco de Mayo

four.Sarah receives a _____ to lighten up

A.Facial

B.Massage

C.Drink

D. Energy Drink

5.Why is Sarah involved?

A.Because she is absolutely too under the influence of alcohol to strain

B.Because she is stuck in a ditch

C.Both A and B

D. None of the above

6.Where is Sarah in search of to go?

A.To her mother-in-regulation's house

B.To a picnic

C.To choose-up her son at a party

D. To Seattle. WA

7.Who is the primary person Sarah meets on the road?

A.Steve

B.John

C.Liam

D. Myrna

eight.Who entails assist Sarah?

A.The Neighbors

B.The Police

C.The Fire Department

D. All of the Above

nine.How antique is Sarah's Youngest Child?

A: 16

B: 11

C: thirteen

D: 21

10.Why does Sarah realise she wasn't being dealt with like she have become susceptible?

A: She sees her car on wheels

B: She punches the firefighter to say thanks

C: The network Priest came to bless her

D: Both A and B.

Chapter 14: The SQ3R Method and Your Reading Log

SQ3R

There is greater to being an effective reader than pace. Comprehension has been pressured at some stage in this e-book. The SQ3R method is a incredible way to double-take a look at your expertise of complicated textual content.

SQ3R stands for Study, Question, Read, Recite/wRite, Review. It grow to be first delivered by the use of Francis Pleasant Robinson in 1946. It is as effective a tool for reading nowadays because it have become 70 years inside the beyond. Let's harm down the acronym:

Study: This is a few difficulty you've already found on this e-book. It is surveying the ebook. Read the economic disaster pick out, sub-titles, any boldface or italicized terms. Get a highbrow concept about what it's miles you'll be reading.

Question: Create a list of questions you have got approximately what your surveying showed you?

• What is the financial disaster approximately?

• Who is mentioned, if everyone, on this financial ruin?

• How does this bankruptcy relate to my task? The course I am taking? My personal growth?

• How will this information benefit me?

By having a set of questions BEFORE you really observe the chapter, you may routinely be seeking out unique statistics even as you are analyzing. This step will also help increase your studying fee.

Read: Now that you've been training to examine faster AND have prepared to take a look at a particular document, your first studying have to provide you with all of the important records to be gained from the file.

Recite/wRite: Whether you're taking notes or orally evaluation, this step is answering the questions you had earlier than you study. There can be one or more particular crucial information you observed that you hadn't idea approximately as well. Remember to maintain a list of the facts.

Review: Time to have a look at for the test. If you've been growing your price, schooling daily, and use the SQ3R technique to have a study an important and complex file, reviewing ought to be smooth thinking about you have got were given reviewed it numerous times thru now.

Chapter 15: Into The World Of Speed-studying

Reading brings our eyes, mouth, mind, and ears to existence; it stimulates those vital senses. It moreover enhances brainpower alongside the way.

To Speed-look at Is to See

In analyzing, everything starts offevolved offevolved with the aid of visually decoding the phrases at the net web web page, however how do you precisely look at the phrases at the equal time as you test? Back then, researchers were happy that human beings observe one single word at a time. They believed that we bypass our eyes all through the web page from the left difficulty to the proper, digesting one word after some other. This completely explains how readers have no trouble identifying terms at a faster than everyday fee.

In fact, anybody (except oldsters which can be just beginning to discover ways to study) has the functionality to take a look at greater and at a quicker rate. As we weave through the internet web page, we usually leap into fits and starts offevolved, reading a phrase (or multiple them) in short glances. It is inside the ones brief glances stand the inspiration of pace-studying. You understand this as you pass approximately reading numerous phrases in jus a single look, except of route on the equal time as you encounter phrases that you are surprising with. You furthermore expand your vision unconsciously in an try to examine and apprehend multiple terms in a single look.

To Speed-take a look at Is to Read Silently

While analyzing, you commonly normally tend to talk the phrases to yourself because of the fact you are used to studying them via the "sound-it-out" concept. Back at school, your teacher constantly knowledgeable you to take a look at phrases thru the usage of sounding the letters and their combos. Having that potential to sound out the phrases is an essential skills for each starting reader.

This method slows you down however. You now examine as speedy as you can talk (we call this vocalization) and not on the fee of that you assume, and there's a huge difference. Saying the words, even whispering them internal your thoughts can also take time, however that is the manner you pace-study.

Speed-analyzing Is Also Comprehending

People check because of the reality they want to comprehend what they observe. How well they comprehend what they're reading depends now not only on their analyzing speed, but additionally on their vocabulary and familiarity with the concern depend.

Speed-analyzing normally will growth your studying comprehension. Since you look at a couple of phrases at one time, you benefit the capability to recognise the words' that means in context. It improves your great knowledge and vocabulary, and in flip will growth your reading pace as properly.

...and Concentrating

Reading calls for interest, but in case you have interaction in tempo-analyzing, you want to display forceful and sustained hobby – you do many stuff on the equal time on the identical time as at it. Effective pace-reading manner you ought if you want to take a look at down the terms even as closing alert to what the aspect/book's author desires to impart to you, particularly records how the fabric is obtainable so you can absolutely realize the principle thoughts at the identical time. Once that is completed you begin to observe rapid with a better mind-set.

Chapter 16: Speed-analyzing Techniques To Improve Reading Speed And Comprehension

Read Early

Individuals can enhance their interest and growth their studying tempo through using analyzing crucial materials early in the day. It moreover allows masses to prioritize your analyzing. Categorize your analyzing materials from the least to the most vital, and examine them because of this. Doing so clears and sharpens your mind, consequently improving your comprehension within the tool. You'll moreover take a look at how your studying speed is considerably superior.

Practice Skimming the Material First for Relevant Ideas

Aim to rush-observe nonfiction works, collectively with educational texts and the way-to books for fundamental thoughts. Scanning the desk of contents, or reading every paragraph's first and ultimate sentences may be the first rate way to do it. Understanding the structure of the fabric first is crucial; you'll have a higher idea which portions to skim and which quantities to study more carefully.

Questions?

Another powerful pace-analyzing technique is probably to expose headings and subheadings of your reading substances into questions. This lays the inspiration where you may now begin scanning the whole text for solutions. In addition, as you intensely interest on the cloth, you unconsciously beautify your studying velocity and comprehension.

Reading inside the Right Environments

Yes, you could take a look at pretty lots anywhere you want and but you want. This is what makes reading so fun and worthwhile.

However, propping your e-book using a bookstand and angling it at forty five stages to make the studying revel in as cushty as viable, notably improves reading velocity. Such analyzing consolation reduces eyestrain as nicely. When tempo-studying, it might do you genuine to refrain from studying critical (or difficult) materials in bed, because your frame and mind are already in a cushty state. Reading collectively in conjunction with your ebook on a desk as a substitute makes you alert maximum of the time.

The Case of Highlighting

Many readers do not forget that highlighting terms in yellow (which includes wonderful shades) complements their reading pace/comprehension. Unfortunately, this isn't always the case. To highlight the phrases truely approach you may as an alternative pass them for now on the equal time as studying. It received't be long in advance than you be aware that you have to take a look at the cloth two times. It could possibly moreover be viable which you won't understand or perhaps go through in thoughts them.

Preview Before Reading

Look thru your reading materials first in advance than settling down. This ought to give you an superb feel of the critical and thrilling additives. This moreover tells you quantities that you may bypass so that you need to attention greater on those important additives.

Your Flexible Reading Speed

There are studying materials that want to be have a look at slowly and with care (poetry, mathematical equations, and especially crook contracts). Then there's the amusing stuff you may have a look at with pace: novels, magazines, and newspapers. It might be smart to adjust how fast you have got a take a look at great studying substances.

Chapter 17: You May Have Yet To Realize It Now, But Speed-studying Boosts Your Productivity

That's right. Speed-analyzing is an important time-control talent that improves productivity. This can also furthermore seem a simple tactic that does some wonders at an thoughts-set, however it's extra of a method, that when practiced, will present large dividends in the manner you discern to your targets. If you're able to take a look at and digest content material cloth material quicker than you could plan and act effectively; you stay one step in advance most of the time. In addition, velocity-studying can be very crucial in improving your productivity and your career in substantial.

There's no denying how we are all enthusiastic about standard overall performance and productivity in recent times. So lots emphasis is implanted on such tendencies that the mind are overused, and alongside the way, the phrases have already out of place part of their meanings. Even if such mind aren't without a doubt used as they should be, the requirements concerned nonetheless stay in region, and it's far vital to determine out the manner to stay efficient and inexperienced in our every day lives, especially at the same time as we're surrounded by means of the use of distractions. This is wherein simple methods (however with profound blessings whilst treated as a protracted-term technique) such tempo-studying to loose up time and stay a step in advance of the game counts.

Most human beings often have a take a look at 250 to three hundred phrases in line with minute. If you want to face out from some of the rest with the aid of reading and operating in the direction of powerful speed-studying strategies, you'll double the fee with which you have a look at quite actually, or even study quicker than that.

The capability to rush-look at is also vital whilst doing research. You'll be able to get for your objectives rapid clearly thru skimming the materials earlier than you efficiently.

To employ pace-analyzing exercise making fewer eye stops. Train your eyes to limit the stops (particularly the time taken for the period of every prevent) they make as you have a look at terms in a line. Each shop you can additionally most effective take a fragment of a 2d, however with severa stops along the road, the time out of region turns into enormous. It will have an impact to your reading pace.

You additionally have this tendency to back-skip (others fancily name it regression) as you observe about. Looking lower back on the items you truly have a look at (be it consciously or unconsciously) because you possibly have misread it, or did not recognize it, no longer nice continues you from analyzing fast sufficient, it also reduces your comprehension. While lower once more-skipping is a healthy exercise, you want to do it for top motives. As you adhere for your velocity-reading strategies, you furthermore might also lessen the temptations to yet again skip.

It also permits to appearance multiple phrases. Condition your mind to look and recognize as many phrases as you can before transferring on. Try to start as an extended way away as you can easily see through the road even as anchoring your eyes to the primary phrase of the line. You also can exercise the equal approach to the phrase resting on the give up of the road.

Chapter 18: The Idea That You Can Learn To Read three hundred% Faster In Just 6 Hours

How powerful need to you be if you can collect all of your required analyzing in best a third of the time it usually takes to achieve this? You have to best be given as authentic with the opportunities and potentials.

To boom your analyzing tempo is nothing more than a technique of having manage of your incredible motor movement. Experiments designed to permit us human beings to examine quicker at a given time have efficaciously produced common will increase of as a good deal as a whopping three hundred%, and even more. The basis of such experiments is the ideas that signify the human visible tool. Through data how the tool works, we must eliminate our inefficiencies and enhance our functionality to hurry-take a look at (and decorate retention as properly) as a substitute.

The technique calls for minimizing the fixations (and their durations) consistent with line to stimulate studying at a faster-than-ordinary tempo. Here, we are introduced to the idea of reading through a sequence of saccadic actions (or jumps) in choice to usually analyzing in immediately traces. Each saccade ends with a fixation, a few like to call it a brief image of all the phrases in the focused region. The fixation should have to very last a quarter, or half of a 2d, to untrained subjects. You must enjoy this your self through closing one eye and placing a fingertip above its eyelid. You then slowly take a look at the cloth in a right away line using your different eye. By doing this you'll find out separate and first-rate moves with durations of fixation.

The discovery (of the possibilities and potentials as a way to study quicker at three hundred% in just 6 hours) rides along beneficial speed-reading techniques which includes disposing of again-skipping and regression. It relies on our capability to make use of conditioning drills that allow us to boom our horizontal peripheral imaginative and prescient span, especially the quantity of phrases so one can be registered for every fixation involved. The showed technique should be applied through conditioning ourselves to the wishes and specs before we can start trying out our pace-analyzing competencies (approximately 3 times faster than our focused analyzing speed) that includes comprehension.

You start through the usage of figuring out your baseline (that is your contemporary studying velocity). This is carried out thru counting the phrases in any 5 given strains of a e-book. Divide the give up result thru five to get your not unusual word-consistent with-line. Next, decide the common traces for each page thru counting text traces on 5 separate pages. Divide the surrender result yet again via five, which you should then multiply with the not unusual phrase-in keeping with-line. What you presently have is your commonplace word-in line with-web page.

Using a timer, look at via your fabric for 1 minute. Read and comprehend – study at your normal tempo. Then multiply what number of traces make up your not unusual word-steady with-line so you can decide your phrase-in step with-minute fee.

As stated above, doing away with regression and back-skipping is an crucial speed-studying component. With that already settled, you may now reputation on the subsequent section of your tempo-studying transition – perceptual enlargement. Try zeroing in on the middle of a computer display show and also you'll phrase how you may though visualize and register its additives properly. Training your peripheral imaginative and prescient to perceive and sign up efficiently will boom your studying tempo to about 3 hundred%, even greater.

Once you get snug with this, you can now compute your new word-in line with-minute analyzing speed. Read thru for 1 minute – check as speedy as you can recognize.

Determine what number of traces to procure and multiply the result collectively with your previous commonplace phrase-in keeping with-line to achieve at your new phrase-in keeping with-minute price.

Chapter 19: How You Should Speed-Read

Learning a way to rush-study need to not be a burden. You need to begin via manner of showing flexibility and staying power into this challenge.

Make Good Use of Hand Techniques

Train your forefinger to transport under traces of phrases rapid sufficient on your eyes to have a look at. Then waft it all of the manner proper down to the primary phrase in the next line as brief as you could. This specific method ought to assist manual your eyes as you pace-look at your way thru.

Relax While At It

It is crucial which you discover ways to lighten up and pay hobby on the equal time as pace-studying on the same time. A relaxed country facilitates to hold you centered on digesting records at the words you simply study, and now not totally on the act of reading fast itself. This takes time and exercise of path, however you'll get there ultimately. Just bear in mind that comprehension is important for everything which you observe – do no longer study at a remarkable rapid tempo if you cannot apprehend or consider the content fabric.

Doing Away With the Spoken Word

Stop thinking about the "spoken word." You might not mouth the terms in silence as you take a look at via, however opportunities are that you keep in mind (or subvocalize) the terms you spoke aloud. It also can additionally are available in handy even as reading difficult texts, however it is going to be useless at the equal time as velocity-studying. Make it a dependancy to prevent yourself every time it takes place. If you are used to transport your lips as you observe, close to them using your hands till you save you the addiction.

Swallow In Groups Of Words

The key's to stop studying every phrase one after the other. Read and realise groups of phrases on the equal time. This takes a great deal a lot much less eye motion, allowing you to examine loads quicker as an alternative.

It Helps to Find a Well-Lit and Quiet Environment

You may be capable of study better irrespective of historical past track or inner crowded coffee stores. But if such distractions are minimized, you'll gain greater tempo-analyzing wonders. If you can't discover a quiet environment to relax into (studying in bed is not the solution), you can always use earplugs to block out the distractions.

Make It a Point to Read Whenever You Are Alert and Engaged

It's a fact that humans function nicely at some stage in mornings. Others have tested themselves to anticipate hundreds higher sooner or later of afternoons. Ask yourself in that you are maximum comfortable with, and have a look at away.

Chapter 20: Speed-Reading And Comprehension Goes Hand In Hand

Reading rapid and comprehending what you have a look at is the overall package deal deal deal. If you fail to realize what you observe in a brief tempo then you simply advantage now not some thing. Focus to your studying comprehension as well. To do this, velocity-take a look at whilst the day is still more younger. This is wherein your concentration is at its greatest; you'll moreover hold more of the information gathered than at the same time as analyzing in the direction of middle of the night.

A actual tip to decorate your comprehension might be to take a look at out for short bursts. Reading for 30 to forty mins and taking breaks afterwards flexes your thinking. The breaks allow time if you want to truly digest the content material which you virtually have a have a look at and reputation on the cloth available. This is extraordinary performed in a quiet surroundings in which there is lots much less distraction.

While at it, strive to reveal your comprehension improvement as properly. Ask your self what you've got found out along the manner. If you seem to have problem answering the query, re-check the fabric. You can also ask someone that will help you understand the content material fabric material.

Annotate

Be active via underlining, circling – make well-known notes alongside the lines. You additionally need to make you very personal manual so that you can effortlessly distinguish vital devices that want in addition hobby. This also keeps you in keeping with the goals of the content material that you simply look at. Skim the chapters first – be aware about discover pages, subtitles, the introductions and bankruptcy summaries in advance than attractive the whole financial ruin.

What Skimming Brings to the Table

Without a doubt, skimming has a looming impact on comprehension. You have to now not lodge to skimming on every occasion your purpose is the whole comprehension of the content cloth you're approximately to look at. Skimming is great used whilst coming across, or getting the textual content's ordinary concept.

Nonetheless, at the same time as jogging with restrained time, skimming over the textual content can beneficial resource your comprehension. When as compared to everyday reading, and given enough time to browse via typically, the primary thoughts of whole texts are higher understood while you resort to skimming, in contrast to everyday analyzing.

In evaluation, there are studies made that suggest how high quality tempo-reading courses that maintain forth about techniques in large element primarily based mostly on skimming over written texts have resulted to a fairly decrease comprehension rate. Even critics of the velocity-studying practice believed that to speed-look at is to skim, and now not to take a look at.

Chapter 21: How To Read Fast, And Efficiently

Why?

Think approximately it. Think about how lots analyzing you often do on a every day basis. Your first prevent within the mornings can be the newspaper so that you'll apprehend what's occurring the arena in recent times. Then you pass on into emails from paintings and co-workers. Later on, you discover yourself digging into books, critiques, letters, and hints that make up your commonplace day.

Looking at it, studying must nicely be our most used artwork-associated talent. It's that important. And we take it with no consideration.

That must not be the case. Given the impact analyzing has on our each day lives and careers, it is a capability we want to preserve to improve.

What does it advocate to end up a higher, powerful reader but? It virtually approach reading faster and records the content material material cloth at the equal time. It moreover method removing your awful analyzing behavior so that you make the most your tempo-reading prowess to boost your productiveness.

How We Read

How do you study without a doubt? How do you're making feel of the letters within the phrases and their shapes, and setting they all together to make a sentence you can apprehend?

Bluntly positioned, studying is a complex skills. Experts accept as genuine with that every of our eyes is able to locking onto amazing letters and emblems (characters aside) on the equal time. Your mind robotically fuses the pics to form the arena you are studying. Such interest occurs right away as we pass approximately zipping thru the pages.

Inefficient Eye Motions

In the case of slow readers, they usually commonly tend to focus unconsciously on each word that passes through them, slowly working their manner through every line. The human eye has that ordinary capability to span as a great deal as at the least one.Five inches at any time, which already covers about four to 5 phrases.

Following this, there may be additionally the perception that readers generally do now not rely on their peripheral vision to recognize the phrases at every edges of a line.

Overcoming this is easy. Ease up for your gaze as you have a look at. You can do that through retaining your face comfortable as you increase your gaze. The quit end result may be your new ability to view blocks of words. Gone are the instances at the same time as you note each word one after the other. Once you switch out to be snug with the workout, your eyes will instinctively skip across the net net web page at a miles faster rate than the equal antique. And as you close to every line's stop, your peripheral imaginative and prescient will maintain on with the aid of honestly going during the last devices of phrases.

The idea of Meta Guiding

This method dwells at the concept of visually guiding the human eye the usage of hints (a incredible example is a pen, or your finger) to make it pass quicker alongside rows and rows of terms in books. If you want to have interaction in velocity-reading, your eyes have so one can keep up with the desires of the exercising. Meta guiding consists of illustrating invisible shapes on a text with the purpose of broadening the visible span. This must help you put together for speed-studying.

A correct instance might be the use of your finger or pen to make shapes on a positive web page with the concept that the method could stimulate our visible cortex, because of this developing your visible span to recognise the complete line, and going to the quantity of imprinting the information internal your unconscious so you can also additionally retrieve it later. Meta guiding is also believed to have decreased sub vocalization, speeding your studying instead. It encourages your eye to chorus from skimming over the content fabric, which only reduces comprehension and your potential to make appropriate use of your reminiscence.

Your Speed-reading Success

Learning "how" to hurry-look at is honestly the primary phase. You are going to need to condition each your bodily and intellectual self to end up ideal at it. Practice (and extra exercising) is the most critical component proper right here. Use this capability frequently. It took you a number of years to discover ways to have a look at. It will also take you another precise amount of years to improve how you read.

As you begin to pace, it's vital to do not forget the schooling and tips already cited above and positioned them into movement. And on the identical time as at it, report the development of your cutting-edge studying tempo so you can gauge the outcomes and impact of your practices and drills. You can make use of severa on line pace-reading assessment net web sites for this.